For Permission Requests,
Write To The Publisher At The Address Below:

JVB Consults LLC
458 North Doheny Drive. #69189
West Hollywood, CA 90048

(E) info@jvbconsults.com

───────────────────────────

International Standard Book Number (ISBN)
979-8-218-52374-9

Library of Congress Control Number (LCCN)
2024920263

The Blessing Of Transition:
FINDING STRENGTH IN CHANGE

The Blessing Of Transition:

FINDING STRENGTH IN CHANGE

Dedication

To the younger Jordan,

Thank you for your tenacity and unwavering spirit, for the courage to remain true to yourself even when the world seemed determined to dim your light. Your strength and resilience have become the very foundation upon which I stand today, guiding me through every twist and turn of this journey. You are the heartbeat of this memoir.

To the teachers and mentors who graced my path,

This journey is as much yours as it is mine. Your wisdom, patience, and unwavering support illuminated the darkest corners of my life, helping me navigate the challenges that often felt insurmountable. You were the guiding stars, always present when I needed a light to find my way.

To my dear cousin, Sierra Watties,

Though you departed this earth far too soon, your presence in my life was a gift beyond measure. During my hardest times, you were a beacon of love and understanding, reminding me of who I was and what I was meant to do in this life. It's because of you that I found the willpower to sit down and write this memoir. You not only reignited my purpose but also reminded me of a truth that I carry with me: people often think they know you—all of you—without ever having truly met you or knowing the full depth of your story. *"No one can tell your story but you,"* you said. And so, here I am, sitting down to tell it.

Learning of your passing made me reflect on the many others who have left this earth too soon. It was a stark reminder of life's fragility and unpredictability. I knew then that I had to tell my story—not just for myself, but in the hopes of reaching others who may find solace in these words.

This memoir is my heart laid bare, an unapologetic journal of my life. It captures the essence of the younger Jordan, preserving the memories and the lessons that have shaped my journey. It's why, at the end of each chapter, I've included *"The Transition Unveiled & The Blessing Embraced."* Where I am now in life, I've come to understand that telling your story is not just about processing and feeling it; it's about recognizing the lessons within each experience. Just like with any journal, you look back, you reflect on what happened, and you ask, *"What was the lesson here? What was the universe trying to reveal to me?"* This is my way of embracing each transition and uncovering the blessings they have brought into my life.

A Note On The Absence Of Traditional Chapter Titles

As you turn the pages of this memoir, you may notice something missing—traditional chapter titles. I've chosen to forgo these familiar markers in favor of a more authentic and organic approach. Instead of overthinking beautifully crafted titles, each section of this memoir is marked by the year it represents, mirroring the way life unfolds—one year at a time.

Why no chapter titles? Because life doesn't come to us neatly wrapped in poetic or perfectly packaged phrases. Up until now, I had never truly sat down with my thoughts to process the full weight of my life's experiences. And when I did, I realized that creating clever or elaborate chapter titles felt like trying to romanticize something that was raw, real, and deeply personal. Some years don't arrive with beautifully named lessons; sometimes, they show up as, *"What the hell just happened?"*

This memoir is not just a recounting of years but a reflection of how life happens—in its messy, unpredictable, and profoundly human way. By anchoring each chapter to a specific year, I hope to invite you into my story with the same authenticity that shaped it. Life doesn't hand us tidy titles; it hands us moments, lessons, and opportunities to grow. And that's exactly how I've chosen to share my journey with you.

The Blessing Of Transition:

FINDING STRENGTH IN CHANGE

Contents

Journal Entry

1986 – 1991

Every child enters the world as a blank canvas, untouched by the colors and strokes that life will eventually bring. They arrive, not by choice, but by the natural order of life, with no understanding of the world they are born into. In those first moments, a child's mind is an empty expanse, waiting to be shaped and guided by those who hold the brush to their future.

I, *Jordan Van Allen Brown*, was born on August 9, 1986, at 9:47 AM at Union Memorial Hospital in Baltimore, Maryland. As the seconds turned into minutes and the minutes into hours, a new canvas was unfurled, ready to be painted by the experiences and influences that would soon follow.

In 1987, at one, I was a small yet curious observer of the world around me. My mother often remarked on how I seemed to take in everything with wide, attentive eyes, absorbing my surroundings even before I could fully understand them. By 1988, at two years old, the canvas was gradually being touched by the hands of those around me—my mother, family, sibling—each leaving an impression, whether I was aware of it or not.

In 1989, I was three years old. The world was still vast and unknown, but my brain was beginning to awaken, slowly piecing together the sights, sounds, and sensations that would form the foundation of my earliest memories. By 1990, at four years old, the colors on the canvas became more vibrant, more defined, as my mind continued to develop, taking in the world with a growing sense of awareness.

Then came 1991. I was five years old, and it was as if the light had finally begun to shine through. My brain, once dormant, now stirred with the first flickers of understanding. The blank canvas was no longer blank. It was becoming a tapestry of early memories, emotions, and experiences—though still in its infancy, it was beginning to tell a story.

These early years, though distant and hazy, laid the groundwork for the person I would become. They were the first strokes on the canvas of my life, guided by the hands of those around me, shaping the foundation of who they thought I would become today.

Journal Entry

1992

By 1992, my mind was beginning to awaken, and the world around me was coming into sharper focus. I was six years old, living on Rogers Avenue in Baltimore, Maryland, in a spacious, beautiful home. My sister and I had ample room to explore, create, and revel in the boundless imagination that childhood brings. The house was grand, but I remember it being sparsely furnished, with rooms that felt open and uncluttered, spaces my mother tried her best to fill with warmth and comfort.

My father was often in and out, a presence that was both familiar and distant. I was told it was because of work, but even at that young age, I wondered if there was more to it.

I looked forward to Sunday mornings because I knew it was time to hear some wonderful music and connect with other kids who were also attending the service. My mother was deeply religious, a devout believer in God, and we attended an Apostolic church with unwavering regularity. We would all pile into our white station wagon and drive to church, gospel music filling the car. My mother, dressed in a long skirt that modestly covered her knees, wore no makeup and no nail polish—her adherence to the strict Apostolic doctrine. When I asked her why she dressed that way, she explained that it was the Apostolic way, what they were taught. Women were not permitted certain liberties, a concept that seemed foreign to me but one I didn't question at the time.

There was something about a Black church—the way everyone was dressed, the music that poured out of the storefront church. I could hear it as we parked our car, and I could even smell the wood of the chairs as we approached the door. I would sit in the congregation, playing my favorite tambourine as hard as I could, lost in the fervor of the music. The church choir, with their powerful and soulful voices, stirred something within me that I couldn't quite comprehend.

Tears would stream down my face, moved by the music in a way that was beyond words. Even at that tender age, I understood the power of music, the way it could reach into the depths of my soul and bring forth emotions I didn't know existed.

As we drove home from church, I would often beg my mom to turn on the gospel station. I knew the melodies would comfort me the same way they did in church. I don't know why, but, I wanted to take those church feelings home with me. At home, I began to sing— constantly. Music became my sanctuary, a source of joy and solace. My father noticed this whenever he was around, and for Christmas that year, he gifted me my first karaoke machine. It is still a vivid memory, the way the machine would light up with the intensity of my singing, the lights growing brighter the louder I sang. It became my favorite possession, and I would spend hours singing, pouring my heart into each note. Music soon became my comfort, my protector.

My sister and I shared a unique bond. She was soft-spoken and very observant, not naturally drawn to the energetic bursts that defined my days. I think my sister would have enjoyed staying in her room, being to herself. But I couldn't let her do that; I wanted her to be my partner in crime. I was always finding ways to coax her out of her shell, to make her laugh and join in on the fun. We had this big basement, practically empty, making it the perfect space for our adventures. Often, we would put on our roller skates and glide across the basement floor to the tunes of gospel music. It was our little world, just the two of us, spinning and laughing until we were breathless. Then we'd race back upstairs, still giggling, to grab something to eat. Those moments were special, and I felt like I brought out the best in her during that time.

Music was my everything. But, when gospel music no longer seemed to touch me in the way I needed, I began to explore other genres, discovering new sounds and voices that spoke to different parts of my soul. I would mimic the singers I admired, their voices becoming a part of my own as I sang along with my karaoke machine. My father, though not always present, was my biggest fan. Whenever he came home, he would encourage me to get out my karaoke machine and sing for him. He allowed me to express myself freely, never questioning the femininity that sometimes crept into my performances. He nurtured my spirit, letting me be who I was without judgment.

But it wasn't always easy. My mother, devout in her beliefs, would sometimes chastise me, telling me that boys shouldn't act that way, shouldn't sing like that. It was confusing, this push and pull between my parents—my father encouraging me to be myself, my mother trying to mold me into what she believed was right. She would often urged my father to engage me in more traditional masculine activities. Asking him to bring out toy trucks and airplanes, to play basketball and football with me in our beautiful, well-maintained backyard. But my heart wasn't in it. My soul was happiest when I was singing, when I was lost in the music that flowed from my beloved karaoke machine.

At six years old, I didn't have the words to describe what I was feeling, but I knew there was something powerful happening within me. The music, the church, my parents—all were shaping me in ways I didn't fully understand. Even at that young age, I often wondered if the church was brainwashing my mother, if my father was wrong for encouraging my free spirit, if the music was changing me in ways I couldn't control. Everything seemed too much to comprehend all at once. But one thing was certain: I would never let go of that rainbow karaoke machine. It was more than just a toy; it was a lifeline, a connection to something deeper within myself that was just beginning to awaken.

The Transition Unveiled & The Blessing Embraced

1992 was a year of awakening. The music, the church, and the contrasting influences of my parents began to carve out the contours of my young identity. The blessing here was in the discovery of music as my sanctuary—a lifeline amidst the confusion and the rigid expectations around me. It was through this early connection with music that I began to find my voice, a voice that offered comfort and clarity in a world that often seemed uncertain. The tambourine in church, the karaoke machine at home, and the melodies that lingered in my mind all spoke of a freedom that was just beginning to unfold, hinting at the deeper journey of self-expression that lay ahead.

1993

First grade was an uncharted territory for my seven-year-old self in 1993. It was a time of discovery, where my young mind started to piece together the intricacies of the world around me, like filling in the details of that blank canvas at birth. We lived in a beautiful white-painted home near Pimlico Racetrack on Rogers Avenue in Baltimore, Maryland. This house was more than just four walls; it was a world of its own, a place where my mother, my sister, and I found solace.

To reiterate, the space felt expansive and open, a home where we could express ourselves freely and explore the wonders of childhood. My sister and I, despite having different fathers, shared the unwavering love of our mother. Her love was a constant, knitting together our small family with a strength that was palpable even at my young age.

Our neighborhood was quiet, almost serene, lined with large, dignified houses that stood like silent sentinels. The air was usually filled with a sense of calm, broken only on weekends by the buzz of the races at Pimlico. The racetrack brought a kind of magic to our otherwise tranquil street. On race days, the neighborhood transformed. The streets would fill with cars, and well-dressed people in their finest attire would gather, drawn to the spectacle of the horses. I remember watching them from our front porch—their elegance and excitement fascinated me, painting a picture of a world so different from ours. My mother would often mention the races in passing, her tone a mix of curiosity and distance. It was a world we observed from afar, a swirl of glamour and excitement that seemed just out of reach. I accepted this quietly, understanding in my own way that some things were not meant for us.

Our home, though large and inviting, sometimes gave the impression that it was shared. I soon discovered, it was a duplex—a massive house that had been divided, with each resident having their own entrance. Our neighbors occupied the entire top floor, while my mother, my sister, and I occupied the middle floor and the basement. Despite this proximity, we rarely interacted with the neighbors. Our lives were separate, each family carving out their own space within the house. The driveway often held more than one car, confirming the presence of others, but our paths never really crossed. Inside our space, my sister and I made use of every corner. The backyard was our playground, a vast expanse of lush green grass that stretched out endlessly, giving us the freedom to run, play, and dream. It was here, amidst the sprawling greenery, that some of my most cherished memories were made. My father, who was still often in and out of our lives, was at the center of many of those memories.

His presence was a whirlwind of joy that I eagerly welcomed and truly loved. He would arrive with a smile that could light up the room and a warmth that made the world feel just a little bit safer. My father's visits were unpredictable, but they were also magical. We would spend hours in the backyard building paper planes, launching them into the sky with laughter that echoed through the yard.

In those moments, nothing else mattered. I didn't understand why he wasn't always around. The reasons for his absence remained a mystery, an unanswered question that lingered at the edges of my awareness. When he was there, life felt full, like a story that was just beginning. And yet, there was always a part of me that wondered why he had to leave, why our time together was always cut short. Still, I held onto the joy of his presence, hoping it would never end.

But those days were fleeting, a fact I would soon come to realize in the most heartbreaking way.

I had no idea that the rhythm of his visits, the pattern I had grown to cherish, would soon be shattered. The day it all changed arrived with a jarring abruptness. It was July 6, 1993. The memory of that day is etched into my mind like a scar. It began with a scream—a scream so raw and piercing that it seemed to split the air in two. My sister and I were inside the house when we heard our mother cry out, a sound that came from the depths of her soul. In an instant, everything shifted. The house, which had always been our safe haven, filled with an overwhelming sense of chaos and sorrow.

Within minutes, women from the church, close friends, and even mere acquaintances flooded our home. They moved with a purpose, surrounding my mother, who was consumed by grief. I vividly remember one of the women gently took my sister and me upstairs, away from the commotion. She tried to reassure us, telling us not to worry, that our mother was just in emotional pain. But even at seven, I knew this was more than just emotional pain. I could feel the gravity of the situation settling in the pit of my stomach, a sensation that made it hard to breathe. As we sat upstairs, I listened to the muffled sounds of crying and praying from below, the voices blending into a haunting melody of despair.

Through the upstairs window, I watched as more people gathered outside. They stood in clusters, some crying, others with their hands clasped in prayer, their faces a mixture of sorrow and resolve. I wanted to ask what was happening, to demand answers, but I was frozen by the fear of the unknown. It wasn't until later, when the crowd had begun to thin, that I saw my grandmother—my father's mother—arrive. Her presence added a new weight to the day, a solemnity that deepened the already heavy atmosphere. She walked up to my mother and, in a voice that trembled with emotion, said words that I have carried with me ever since: *"Although he's gone, he left me with words to tell you."* My grandmother went on to explain that my father had entrusted her with a final request—that she would take care of the children he left behind.

He had spoken those words to her, knowing that if anything ever happened to him, it would be his mother's duty to ensure his children were cared for.

In that moment, the reality settled in. My father was gone. The man who had brought laughter into our home, who had made me feel seen and cherished, was no longer a part of this world. The paper planes we built together, the songs we sang on the rainbow karaoke machine, all became relics of a past that I could never return to. With his passing, a piece of my childhood innocence faded, replaced by an early understanding of loss and the fragility of life.

I was left holding onto the memories of just two years with my father. Those two years were not even complete, as his presence was never consistent. The moments we had were like scattered fragments of a dream—a dream that was now forever out of reach. His laughter, his warmth, the way he made everything feel just a little bit brighter, all condensed into brief flashes of time. I realized that I would have to carry those fragments with me, that they would have to sustain me in the years to come. My father had been my anchor, and now, without him, I felt adrift in a sea of uncertainty.

The Transition Unveiled & The Blessing Embraced

The transition in this chapter was the profound loss of my father—a figure who brought light and love into my young life. In the wake of his departure, I was forced to confront a world that felt less certain, less safe. The blessing, though not immediately apparent, lay in the resilience that began to take root within me. It was in the face of this heartache that I learned the first lessons of strength and the enduring power of the love that remains even after someone is gone.

Journal Entry

1994

The second grade was a time of confusion and searching for answers. My days were filled with school, friends, and the quiet questions that lingered after my father's passing. His absence cast a long shadow over our lives. Every time someone stopped my mother and me to share their condolences, it was a reminder of the void left behind, a constant echo of the life we were now trying to navigate without him.

I was just an innocent child, still learning to process such a profound loss. The joy that I had started to embrace with my father's presence was now gone, and I found myself asking, *"Where will I find this joy now? Where do I look for it? Who has it to offer?"*

Our once happy home, now occupied by three instead of four, felt different. I could see the change in my mother, how she turned to those she trusted, searching for answers just as I was. I believe she too was grappling with the same questions—*where do we find the joy and comfort we once knew?* My mother began to date again, and the men introduced to me never quite filled the void left by my father. It felt as though my mother was searching for someone to pick up where my dad had left off, but even at eight years old, I knew that no one could replace the man who had been there from the start.

As the year progressed, another significant change was on the horizon. Without much explanation, my mother decided that we were moving. I never asked why; perhaps I was too young to understand, or maybe I was too afraid of the answers. The beautiful home that I had come to love, the space where I had begun to make my own, was about to be left behind. Losing my father had been hard enough, but now I was also losing the place where I had found a measure of comfort and security.

We moved into a two-bedroom apartment down the street from my aunt, her husband, and their two kids—my cousins. It was smaller, cozier, but it didn't hold the same sense of home that the house on Rogers Avenue had. It was another loss, another piece of the life I had known slipping away. As I settled into our new apartment, I couldn't help but feel that I was leaving behind more than just a physical space. I was leaving behind the last remnants of the life I had shared with my father, the joy we had found together, and the innocence of my early childhood.

The Transition Unveiled & The Blessing Embraced

The transition in this chapter was the move to a new home, symbolizing the loss of both my father and the physical space where I had begun to find comfort. The blessing, though not immediately clear, was the resilience that began to build within me as I learned to adapt to these changes.

Journal Entry

1995

By the time I was nine years old, my life had already seen more change than most children my age could imagine. The move to Northern Village Apartments marked the biggest transition yet, one that I found nearly impossible to embrace. While my sister and mother seemed to accept the new place as just another step forward, for me, it was a loss I wasn't prepared for. The world I had known, filled with the joy of my old room, my beloved karaoke machine, and the comforting presence of my father, was gone.

It may not have been the same experience for my mother and sister, though. Perhaps they felt relief in leaving Rogers Avenue behind, especially my mother, who might have seen our old home as a constant reminder of my father. Maybe my sister was eager for a change as well, excited to start anew in a different environment. I never knew their thoughts fully because, at that age, our feelings often remained unspoken. What I knew for certain was my own discomfort. Northern Village felt like a stark departure from the life we had before, a world that was now out of reach, regardless of what it meant to them.

Northern Village Apartments couldn't have been more different from the home we had left behind. Where was the gated fence, the beautiful green grass, and the big home that had once made me feel safe? The quiet nights on Rogers Avenue, with only the sound of birds chirping, were now replaced by something unfamiliar, something unsettling. We were no longer in that comforting bubble; instead, we were here, in a place that felt foreign to me.

Though our new home was just a 7- to -10 minute walk from my aunt and uncle's house, the difference between their life and ours was striking. They lived in a beautiful three-bedroom home with a lovely pool in the back, a huge backyard, and a concrete patio. It was everything our new place wasn't, and I couldn't understand why we had left what we had behind, especially after my dad's death. I never questioned my mother about the move; perhaps I was too young, or maybe too afraid of the answers. But I found comfort in being close to family, especially my aunt.

My aunt became a source of solace for me during this time. She was outgoing, charismatic, and full of life, traits that reminded me of my dad and made me feel safe. I confided in her often, seeking out her love and validation in a world that had become increasingly confusing. Her home reminded me of the warmth and familiarity that our previous life on Rogers Avenue had once offered. Perhaps my mother wasn't running away from what we had but rather from the memories of my dad that filled that space. And while I couldn't grasp it then, the move may have been her way of trying to protect us and herself from the constant reminders of what we once had.

My aunt ran a daycare out of her home, and while the house was often filled with children during the day, it was the moments after the last child left that I cherished the most. My aunt had a well-versed taste in music, far from the traditional gospel tunes that filled my own home. When the daycare hours ended, she would play her favorite music—songs that were rich, soulful, and full of emotion. Artists like: Rachelle Ferrell, Will Downing, Whitney Houston, Earth, Wind & Fire, Chaka Khan, Stephanie Mills, Aretha Franklin, and

Phyllis Hyman filled the air with their powerful voices and captivating melodies.

Listening to these artists opened up a new world for me. Their music made me feel wise beyond my years, stirring emotions and thoughts that were complex for a child my age. I began to understand, or at least question, the stories they told through their songs—the heartache, the joy, the longing. It made me inquisitive about life, relationships, and the depth of human emotions. Music became more than just sound; it was a language that spoke to the parts of me that were searching for understanding and connection. These melodies made me feel seen, even if I couldn't fully articulate it at the time.

But even as I found comfort in my aunt's home, a new challenge was beginning to emerge. My uncle, my aunt's husband, a deeply religious man, began to take notice of something that had also caught my mother's attention—the femininity in my mannerisms. In 1995, the world was not as it is today. Back then, anything that hinted at homosexuality was looked down upon, condemned as sinful, and viewed as a direct path to hell. My mother and uncle, both devout in their beliefs, saw my behavior as something that needed to be corrected, something that required action.

This was when my uncle and mother agreed that he would conduct Bible studies with me. Every week, we would sit down to read the scriptures, his voice firm and resolute as he guided me through passages he believed would steer me away from my developing feminine mannerisms. They hoped that through this routine, the teachings of the Bible would reshape me, extinguishing any possibility of homosexuality before it could take root. What they didn't realize, or perhaps refused to accept, was that no amount of scripture could change the essence of who I was. Their efforts were born out of fear and misunderstanding, not malice, but they couldn't see that my identity wasn't something that needed correction or eradication.

The Transition Unveiled & The Blessing Embraced

The transition in this chapter was the move to Northern Village Apartments, symbolizing not only a physical relocation but also a deeper shift in my sense of safety and belonging. The blessing, though wrapped in difficulty, was the closeness I found with my aunt, the comfort I discovered in music, and the early understanding that I would need to navigate a world that didn't always accept me for who I was.

Journal Entry

1996

The year 1996 marked my tenth birthday, a time in my life that remains one of the hardest to remember and look back on, even now. It was a year clouded by confusion and longing—a time when I was trying to find my place in a world that seemed increasingly harsh and unwelcoming.

My mother, deeply rooted in her Apostolic faith, struggled to understand the changes I was going through. The church, with its rigid beliefs, represented a cornerstone of the churchgoing Black community, but without my father there to protect the parts of me that felt different, I was left vulnerable to a world that sought to reshape me into something I wasn't.

At ten years old, I didn't have a clear understanding of sexuality, of wanting boys or girls, or even of what it meant to be different. All I knew was that I had lost my father, and in that void, I desperately needed love. For a child, love takes on many forms: safety, protection, mentorship, and guidance. I longed for someone to step into the void left by my father—to offer not just affection but a sense of security, a safe space where I could be myself without fear of judgment.

In my young mind, love meant having someone who saw me, who embraced me as I was, without trying to change or fix me. However, my mother, in her devotion to her faith, seemed more concerned with changing who I was than with embracing me. She often allowed others to dictate the outcome of my identity, leaving me to wonder if she was afraid of who I might become. My mother had a way of listening to people, absorbing their opinions, but then kept things moving without addressing the important issues at hand. As a child, this was both confusing and heartbreaking; her vague and inconsistent reactions gave me mixed emotions about where I stood in her eyes. Her fear of what she couldn't understand became a wall between us— even at that young age.

There was one incident in 1996 that captures the pain and confusion of that year. My bond with my aunt had grown stronger than ever, and I found comfort in our relationship. I was attending Halstead Elementary School, a place that felt like a refuge for my sister and me. We used my aunt's address so we could attend, as it was considered a county school, offering a better environment, better teachers, and better opportunities than the city school we would have attended otherwise. Every morning, my sister and I would walk from our apartment to my aunt's house, where we would meet up with her children—my cousins—and then walk the short distance to school together.

But beneath the surface, I was struggling. I longed for love, for acceptance, and I didn't know how to find it. One morning, on our way to my aunt's house, I stopped at the Exxon gas station and bought over $250 worth of candy. The gas station attendant looked at me with suspicion and asked where a ten-year-old had gotten that kind of money. I lied and told him that my aunt had given it to me, but the truth was, I had taken it from her purse the night before while we were listening to music. It wasn't so much about the candy, rather; it was about trying to buy the love and acceptance I so desperately craved. I was willing to do anything to gain acceptance and love at that age. If that meant buying love through books or candies—things I knew were cherished by children because they were my favorites too—then so be it. At ten years old, I was beginning to learn survival skills (misguided as they may have been), I was seeking love that seemed so out of reach.

The following week, I did it again. This time, I took $175 from my aunt's purse and used it to buy books for everyone in my class at the Halstead Elementary School book fair. I thought that if I could make my classmates happy, maybe they would love me, maybe they would accept me. My plan started to unravel when my principal noticed the amount of money I was spending. The books at the fair weren't nearly as expensive as the sum I had in my possession. She questioned me about why I was buying so many books and where I had gotten the money. My answer wasn't convincing, and soon, my uncle, my mother, and my aunt were all called to the school.

While my aunt, who knew me better than anyone, tried to understand what was really going on, it was my uncle and my mother who ridiculed me the most. In front of my friends, my principal, and anyone within earshot, they blamed my actions on what they believed were the *"demons of homosexuality"* within me. Instead of looking deeper into why I felt the need to buy books for my classmates, they fixated on their fears about my identity. Why didn't my uncle and mother see that I was a child seeking connection, longing for acceptance? The idea of me as someone who needed love was overshadowed by their fears and misunderstandings. Their accusations only deepened my confusion and shame.

Around the same time that all of this was going on, my aunt lost her daycare license, a license she had worked so hard to earn. My aunt was a lover of children—her warmth and nurturing spirit shone through in everything she did. To this day, I don't know the full story of how she lost her license, but I remember seeing the hurt in her eyes. I wanted to be there for her during this time, to offer her the same comfort she had given me so many times. But I also knew that staying at her house meant enduring my uncle's religious beliefs and his relentless criticism of my mannerisms. He saw my feminine characteristics as something that needed to be corrected, something sinful. At ten years old, I didn't understand what was considered *"feminine"* or *"masculine."* I was simply being myself. I yearned to continue my routine of being at my aunt's place, but the atmosphere there had changed. I couldn't stand being in a space where I felt like an outsider, an intruder in what was once my safe-haven.

In the midst of all this, nature became my escape. I loved being outside, exploring the world around me. We had moved to a new apartment, and I found myself longing for our old home, where I could play outside in the lush, green grass. But this new place was different; there was no grass to play on, no space that felt free. I started to explore the neighborhood, hoping to find a sense of freedom in these new surroundings. I tried to make friends, but it wasn't always easy. Some kids sensed my difference—my femininity—and they distanced themselves. Others, however, welcomed me, and among them, I found a friend who became my closest friend.

She was everything I longed for in a friend—kind, charismatic, and full of life. I don't think she even noticed my feminine characteristics, and if she did, she never mentioned them. With her, I could be my authentic self. We laughed, joked, and spent countless hours together, from sunrise to sunset. Our mothers grew close as well, bonding over the friendship that had blossomed between us. In her company, I found a space where I felt understood and accepted.

The Transition Unveiled & The Blessing Embraced

The transition in this chapter was the deepening struggle for love and acceptance in a world that was becoming increasingly unpredictable. The blessing, though hard to see at the time, was the resilience and strength that began to form within me, laying the groundwork for the journey of self-discovery that would follow.

Journal Entry

1997

At eleven years old, the world around me felt increasingly unstable, and my curiosity was starting to run wild. My sister and I continued our daily routine of traveling from Northern Village Apartments to our aunt's home, still attending Halstead Elementary School. But things had changed.

After school, I no longer went to my aunt's house. The love and warmth that had once filled her home had faded, and the bond we shared was fractured. My uncle, who had been the dominant figure in the household—the ruler, in a sense—was gone. He had a commanding presence. Needless to say, my aunt and uncle had filed for divorce. To this day, I don't know all the details, but I believe the loss of my aunt's daycare license might have brought tension into the house. Whatever the reasons, their separation marked the beginning of a new chapter, one filled with uncertainty. My aunt had lost the love of her life, and the grief weighed heavily on her. It was a time of brokenness all around me—my aunt, my mother, and even myself. My aunt had now lost her husband. My mother had lost my father. And I had lost my dad. The two women who had been the pillars of my young life were now dealing with their own losses, and in turn, we were all grappling with this profound sense of absence.

I still had my best friend in Northern Village Apartments, and together we clung to the small joys we could find. For me, that joy was in music. Music had always been my refuge, and now, more than ever, I needed its comfort. I remember telling my best friend that we should create a 'show'. We didn't know exactly what we wanted to do, but we knew we loved to roller skate, and I loved to sing. On Sunday mornings, I would put on my mother's choir robe, the one she had taken from the Apostolic church, and I'd stand in the window, singing gospel music. I longed to feel the love and admiration that I associated with the church choir's performances. When the choir sang at church, the congregation would stand up, clapping and cheering, and I wanted to feel that same outpouring of love since we stopped attending church during this time. My mother's car unfortunately had dead and we were carless.

There was something about the Black church that resonated deeply with me. No matter what trials and tribulations the week had brought, there was a sense of hope and renewal every Sunday. The music and the pastor's sermon offered a kind of strength that helped you face the coming week. It wasn't just the traditional teachings or the rituals—it was the hope that the church gave you to keep moving forward.

My best friend and I made invitations for our 'show' with crayons, slipping them into our neighbors' mailboxes, hoping they would come out to see our one-hour 'show'. We had no idea what we were going to perform, but it didn't matter—we were just kids, and we were desperately searching for joy and love in any way we could.

Amidst the sadness and changes, there were pockets of joy and laughter that I hold onto even now. With my uncle no longer around, that meant those bible studies and other activities he once forced on me, would cease. My aunt's home was now hers and it transformed into a hub of fun and family warmth. It became the place to be. My mom, my sister, my cousins, and even a rambunctious little dog brought so much life to that house. Cookouts became a regular event, and if you know anything about Maryland, you know it's all about seafood. We would indulge in crabs, shrimp, hotdogs, and hamburgers, filling the air with the unmistakable aroma of summer fun. My aunt had a deep love for music, and she always had the best tunes playing, turning her home into a lively, joyful space. Those memories are precious to me. I can still see my mom and my aunt (her sister), sitting together, sharing their stories—stories of love, loss, and the complexities of life. They had both lost the men they loved— my aunt to divorce, my mom to loss of my dad. But in those moments, they found solace in each other's company. My sister, my cousins, and I would play until the day turned into night, often refusing to get out of my aunt's pool. Those were the good times. That house was more than just a building; it was a home of love, laughter, and family.

My best friend's mom added to that joy in my life. She was a single mother, much like my own, but she had this infectious spirit that could light up a room. She was always full of laughter and a sense of adventure, and when she had her Corona beers, you knew things were about to get even more lively. There was an unpredictability about her that was exhilarating. She brought a sense of fun and freedom that made every moment with her an adventure. Those moments offered a brief but needed escape from the chaos and the shadows of grief that lingered around us.

But as 1997 progressed, life became more difficult. The shame of the previous year's events still hung over me, and I couldn't face my classmates. The memory of stealing money from my aunt to buy my friends' love was too much to bear. I kept up the routine of walking from Northern Village Apartments down the hill, but now I avoided the Exxon gas station where I had bought all the candy. The attendant at the gas station would glance at me each time I passed, a silent reminder of what I had done. The weight of everyone knowing about my actions made me uncomfortable, almost suffocated by the judgment I felt from those around me. I would walk to Halstead Elementary as if I were going to class, but instead, I would hide. I would linger in the gymnasium, spend long periods in the bathroom, or stay on the playground well past the time I should have gone inside. It wasn't about being outside the school; it was about being anywhere but in the classroom with my peers.

Despite all of this, I was sure to return to lobby of the school by the end of the day as if I missed nothing. I wasn't going to Northern Village Apartments; instead, I was leaving school with my cousins, returning to their mother's home—my aunt's home. I thought I would give revisiting her home another shot being that my uncle had now departed. She never suspected anything was wrong because I ensured that we kept our routine intact. Whenever I avoided the classroom, I made sure to meet my cousins at the school so we could walk to my aunt's house together.

As the year drew to a close, the consequences of my absences became clear. Fifth grade was supposed to be a milestone, a ceremony marking the transition from elementary school, but I had missed too much. My mother, alarmed by my behavior, reached out to my grandmother—my father's mother—desperate for help. *"Jordan is really acting out,"* she told her. *"He wasn't able to participate in the ceremony. We need to put him in therapy. He's still feeling the grief from losing his father."*

And so, I started therapy at Union Memorial Hospital, where I was placed in psychological classes. It was a confusing time for me, trying to process the grief of losing my father, the shame of my actions, and the instability of constant change. Just as I was beginning to settle into Northern Village Apartments, my mother decided we needed to move, again. The room I had shared with my sister, the place with the red bunk bed that had become a small safe-space for me, was no more. I didn't know where we were going, but I knew that once again, my life was in transition.

The Transition Unveiled & The Blessing Embraced

The transition in this chapter was the culmination of grief, shame, and instability, leading to a search for belonging and understanding in a world that felt increasingly uncertain. The blessing, though buried in hardship, was the beginning of a journey toward healing and self-discovery through therapy and the resilience that would carry me through future transitions.

Journal Entry

1998

Moving again, this time to a beautiful, three-bedroom, three-level house with a basement, main floor, and upstairs, felt like a new chapter. It had a lovely backyard, and for the first time in a long while, it almost felt like home was coming back to us. This place stirred memories of my childhood home—those days filled with laughter, music, and my father's presence. Yet, even with this new space offering a glimpse of that lost comfort, reality remained unchanged. My father was still gone, and the grief and lessons from those years followed us like shadows.

At age seven, I didn't understand how my mother managed to buy such a home, especially without ever owning a car or even prioritizing car, first. My thoughts weren't fixated on finances; instead, I simply pondered how and why. Perhaps it was because my sister and I were growing up, reaching an age where sharing a room was becoming less appropriate. Perhaps, we needed our own spaces to change, to have privacy. Maybe my mother sensed this need for separation between us—a boy and a girl on the cusp of adolescence maybe. In her own way, maybe she was trying to provide what we needed, even if it meant stretching beyond her means.

Choosing a theme for my new room should have been exciting, but instead, it became a source of anxiety. My mother, along with my uncle, had always pushed certain expectations onto me, hurling Bible verses and condemning what they perceived as deviant based on my mannerisms and femininity. The pressure to choose something traditionally masculine like Star Wars or G.I. Joe was palpable. I was scared—scared of my mother's reaction if I chose something that didn't fit into her idea of what a boy's room should look like. And would she even help me decorate if it didn't align with her views? It wasn't just about picking a theme; it was about the fear of stepping outside the narrow box they placed me in. In contrast, my sister's room was decorated with a Mickey Mouse theme, something my mother had chosen. Looking back, I wonder if my sister, who is now openly a lesbian, ever truly wanted such a girly room. I can't say what was in my mother's head at the time, but it makes me think about how children should have the freedom to express themselves and choose what resonates with them, even in something as simple as their room decor. Did my mother unintentionally impose her ideas on my sister as well? These thoughts lingered as I navigated my own need for guidance and self-expression in the space where I was meant to grow up.

As we settled into our new home, tensions between my mother and my aunt surfaced. Maybe it was because of the physical distance that the move introduced, or perhaps there were other issues I didn't understand. Despite the change in location, my school routine became more complicated. My mother didn't have a car, so she relied on my grandmother and my aunt for transportation. Every morning, I took the 44 bus from our new home in the city to my aunt's house, where she, her two children, and I would pile into her blue van for the drive to Loch Raven Academy. This routine quickly became a burden—not just on me, but on my aunt as well. The strain was evident, and I began to feel like an inconvenience.

My mother, meanwhile, was making enormous sacrifices. Working at Bank of America in downtown Baltimore, she juggled early mornings, long commutes, and late nights. Without a car, she would take the bus, catch a cab, or rely on rides from anyone who could help. Her days were a constant hustle—getting up early to leave for work before I even opened my eyes, taking whatever transportation she could find, and returning home only after dark. She couldn't see me off to school or be there when I came home. By the time she finally walked through the door, usually around seven or eight in the evening, there was just enough time for a brief catch-up before she went to bed to repeat it all the next day. Watching her navigate these challenges made me aware, even at twelve, of what it meant for a single Black woman to shoulder everything alone. It was an exhausting cycle, and though I could only grasp so much at that age, I knew my mother was sacrificing more than just her time. She was giving up moments of her own life to build a semblance of stability for us.

By this time in our new beautiful home, we had settled in, and it was starting to resemble the vision my mother had for us. There were moments of joy that vividly stand out to me. We had a lovely front porch with green grass extending before it. I was responsible for maintaining the lawn—cutting the front grass, the side grass, and the backyard. It was something I learned by doing, a chore that symbolized my small contribution to this home we now owned. I remember our Christmases being magical, always with the Jackson 5 Christmas album playing in the background. My mother did everything she could to ensure that my sister and I had wonderful holidays, even if it meant sacrificing her own needs. During this time, I began to truly see the lengths my mother would go to make a way out of no way. It was also when I started to understand the hard work involved in maintaining a home. This was not just another place we were renting; this was ours. The upkeep was our responsibility, and my mother's determination to give us a home—our own home—was a testament to her strength and love.

The Transition Unveiled & The Blessing Embraced

This transition brought me to a new home, a physical manifestation of a fresh start amidst the lingering shadows of past grief and uncertainty. The blessing was the resilience we demonstrated to adapt and find hope in this new beginning, even as challenges of identity and family dynamics continued to unfold.

1999

1999 was a year of intense upheaval and transformation, filled with challenges that tested me in ways I never expected. It began with a significant shift in my education. My mother had informed me that I would not be continuing at Loch Raven Middle School. The decision wasn't easy, but the daily routine had become an exhausting ordeal. Each morning, I had to wake up extra early to catch the 44 bus to my aunt's house. From there, we made our way to school. After school, my aunt would pick us up, and the process of getting back home to the city was equally taxing. This daily journey took a toll on my mother, who was already stretched thin working tirelessly at Bank of America in downtown Baltimore. After much deliberation, my mother and aunt decided that continuing in the county school system was no longer feasible. This meant I had to brace myself for the reality of the city public school system, a reality that felt both foreign and intimidating.

Entering Hamilton Middle School was nothing short of a shock. Everything felt different—the people, the environment, the very atmosphere, and even the food. Gone were the colorful bulletin boards that announced upcoming events and activities, the little touches that brought a sense of excitement to Loch Raven. In Hamilton, the furniture was worn and basic, a stark contrast to the vibrant environment I had known. The classrooms felt like they were barely holding on, with chipped paint and outdated supplies. It was as if I had stepped into a completely different world, one that lacked the warmth and community I was used to. The students were rougher, more critical, and far from welcoming.

It was during this time that I started to comprehend the privilege of attending county public schools versus city public schools. The disparities were glaring, from the quality of the facilities to the availability of resources. I began to understand why my mother had fought so hard to ensure that my sister and I attended county schools in the first place. There was a level of opportunity, safety, and comfort that came with county schools, a stark contrast to the environment I now found myself in at Hamilton. Reflecting on this now, I realize how those early experiences shaped my awareness of the systemic inequalities that existed even within the educational system.

The bullying was relentless. Whether I was changing classes, in the cafeteria, or walking home, the taunts and insults followed me everywhere. Hamilton Middle School was only a ten-minute walk from our new home, but those ten minutes felt like an eternity. The verbal abuse often escalated into physical fights, and the frequency of these altercations became so alarming that my grandmother, my father's mother, decided to pick me up after school each day to ensure I made it home safely. It was humiliating to need that kind of protection, but it was necessary. My grandmother's presence during this time became a lifeline, and our bond deepened as she stepped in to support me when I needed it most.

I had never fought or even been in a fight before my time at Hamilton. It was here that I had to learn to defend myself, something that went against every fiber of my being. I didn't want to fight; it wasn't in my nature. But I quickly realized that in this environment, it was a matter of survival. It was as if the halls of Hamilton demanded a certain hardness, and if you didn't have it, you had to develop it. I remember the fear and anxiety that would wash over me each morning, knowing I had to brace myself for whatever might come my way that day.

Amidst all of this, something unexpected happened: many of the female students at Hamilton Middle School gravitated toward me. I wasn't sure if it was my energy or if they felt some sort of sympathy for what they saw me enduring at the hands of the male students. One female student, in particular, stood out to me. She was warm, kind, and seemed to genuinely care about me. At that time, when I was going through all the turmoil, I believed she could be the best friend I desperately needed.

One day, during lunch, she suggested that we leave school early and go to my house to talk. I knew it wasn't the right thing to do, but the idea of spending time with someone who understood me was too tempting to resist. My mother didn't have a car and relied on my grandmother, buses, cabs, or whoever could pick her up if they could. So, I knew we wouldn't be caught. We walked to my home together, hand in hand, and for a moment, I felt a sense of acceptance. People saw us together, and it felt like I had gained some credibility. When we arrived at my mother's newly purchased home, we went directly to the basement to talk. But soon, the conversation shifted as she began to undress in front of me. She removed her pants first, clearly expecting a reaction, but I felt nothing. Then she took off her top and moved closer, placing my face between her breasts. Despite her attempts to seduce me, there was no spark, no attraction. Realizing my lack of interest, she tried one last thing—she took my hand and placed two of fingers inside her. But even then, I felt nothing. We both understood in that moment that I wasn't attracted to her, and I came to a deeper realization that I wasn't attracted to any female.

This experience added another layer of complexity to an already difficult year. I was still grappling with unresolved grief over my father's death, struggling to adapt to a new and hostile school environment, a new home, and a new neighborhood, and now, confronting the truth about my own identity. It was a realization that, deep down, I had probably known for a while but hadn't fully acknowledged until then.

Just when I thought the year couldn't get any worse, tragedy struck our family, yet again. My grandmother had picked me up from Hamilton Middle School one day, and I went to her home instead of mine. I was in the guest room when I heard my grandmother answer the phone. Her face was a mask of shock when she came upstairs to me. She told me that she had to leave and that I should not leave the house or open the door for anyone. The urgency and fear in her voice startled me; it reminded me all too well of the day when one of the church members had told my sister and me to stay upstairs while my mother received the news of my father's passing. This felt eerily familiar.

After some time, my grandmother returned, but she was different— her mood, her energy. I kept asking her what was wrong, but she didn't disclose anything to me. The expression on her face mirrored the look of loss I had seen on my mother's face years earlier. It wasn't until later that evening when my mother called. She told me I needed to stay with my grandmother for the night and be with her if she needed anything. My mother's voice was shaky, but no one would tell me what had happened.

The next morning, as my grandmother was driving me to Hamilton Middle School, she finally spoke. She told me that my aunt had been brutally murdered, stuffed into a bag, and left to die in her own home. She couldn't believe that three of her children were now gone, leaving only one. She also mentioned how grateful she was that I had stayed with her the previous night. My grandfather, her husband, often worked late hours. He was a workaholic, employed at one of the most powerful manufacturing companies in the world. His job was demanding, and he was often only off on some weekends. I rarely saw him since I was always in church on Sundays and busy during the week. I adored my grandfather, even though when he was home, he was usually exhausted. He wasn't a man of many words; he would just kick back with his glass of whiskey on ice, listen to his country music, a genre I had come to enjoy. Occasionally, we would visit his hometown of Virginia, and I loved those long rides with him.

The news of my aunt's death was a major turning point, a moment that reshaped the already tumultuous landscape of 1999. My grandmother's strength became the anchor I so desperately needed amidst the chaos. Despite her pain and loss, she found the resolve to continue, and her unwavering support gave me a sense of stability that was otherwise absent in my life.

I couldn't understand or comprehend how my grandmother was able to immediately go back to work after this tragedy. She worked at Good Samaritan Hospital as the secretary of one of the most demanding departments within that hospital. I knew that not taking some time off would only apply more stress, but maybe it didn't. All I saw at that age was the power and strength of my grandmother in that moment. I was truly blown away by her strength and tenacity to keep going after losing another child.

Although she kept moving forward, I observed a quiet longing in my grandmother—a desire to now journey to Virginia more often. After losing her third child, it was as if she needed the closeness of family and the comfort of her roots to steady herself. She asked my mother if I could join her, to which my mother agreed knowing that she needed support during this time. My grandfather would attend also when he wasn't working. They shared a bond that felt sacred, and I loved absorbing their connection. Each trip to Virginia was a change of pace and a world apart from what I knew. The open atmosphere stretched for miles, with houses spaced far enough apart that you might not see another for a mile or two. There were no trash trucks making rounds—people burned their waste themselves. Life there was different, almost simpler, and every visit left me learning something new.

The more we went, the more I saw my grandmother beginning to heal, though she never voiced it aloud. It was in her eyes during the five-hour drive down, in the way her spirit seemed lighter with each passing mile. She and my grandfather filled the car with country music, introducing me to songs and artists I'd never heard before. Their love, after more than 30 years of marriage, was unspoken yet palpable—two hardworking people who just understood one another. Down in Virginia, I relished the meals of pork barbecue and macaroni and cheese, the warmth of family gatherings, and the stories my uncles told over glasses of whiskey on ice. Though life down south had its challenges, there was a sense of protection in knowing our family was known and looked out for. Those trips became more than just visits—they were a balm for my grandmother and a window into the love, strength, and resilience that defined her and the world she built around her.

The Transition Unveiled & The Blessing Embraced

The transitions in 1999 were numerous and complex—shifting from county to city school, dealing with intense bullying, coming to terms with my sexual identity, and enduring profound family loss. The blessing, though hidden in pain, was the growing self-awareness and resilience that began to form within me and the deepening bond with my grandmother, who provided the love and support I needed to survive.

Journal Entry

2000

The year 2000 marked three years since we had moved into the beautiful home my mother purchased —a place that had slowly become a sanctuary amidst the chaos of our lives. This year felt like it flew by, perhaps because it was my final year of middle school. I had completed the sixth grade at Loch Raven Middle School, which meant that I only had seventh and eighth grade left at Hamilton Middle School.

With my mother working long hours at Bank of America and often having to travel by bus due to not having a car, my sister and I were frequently left to fend for ourselves. The strain of trying to manage on our own, especially when it came to something as basic as dinner, led to friction that neither of us knew how to handle. My sister was older than me, and while one might think that an older sister would step in, I don't think she was equipped to know how to take on that role or what to do in those moments.

I found myself going to my grandmother's house more often during this time. She had just lost another child, and I sensed that she needed some kind of support. Spending more time at her house felt like a way for both of us to fill a void. During one visit, I remember calling home to ask my mother a question. That's when she told me that I needed to come back because my sister had moved out. She would no longer be living with us and was moving to Tennessee to stay with her dad. The news was shocking and unsettling. I didn't have any idea why my sister was leaving. It was never explained to me, and for a while, I thought it might have been because of the tension between us—the altercations we had been getting into. I carried that weight for some time until I later learned that an altercation between my sister and my mom had occurred. To this day, I'm not privy to the details, but I'm glad I no longer have to carry that burden, knowing it wasn't because of me.

I was actually saddened by my sister's departure, but during that time, it was a pivotal moment because, with my sister no longer in the home, my mom and I became extremely close. It was during those times that she started to open up about all the things that were going on in her life, and we would share very serious conversations on the porch. She truly became my best friend at this time, and ultimately, I became the man of the house because it was just my mother and me.

During this time, my uncle, who had always been a significant presence in my mother's life, began visiting more frequently. My mother and my uncle shared a close bond, one that had been nurtured since birth. He was there at the hospital when I was born, and it was clear from their relationship that his presence was essential to my mother. She even allowed him to name me, giving me his middle name: Van Allen.

Despite not having children of his own, my uncle took a special interest in my sister and me, particularly when it came to our education. He made it a point to try and instill in us the importance of education, perhaps as a way to protect us from the hardships we had already faced. However, I wasn't always receptive to his efforts. I recall one particular visit where he came over to teach me using *Hooked on Phonics*, a popular educational tool at the time. But I was resistant, not because I didn't appreciate his efforts, but because of everything else I was going through. The weight of the past few years had left me emotionally exhausted, and I simply wasn't in the right space to engage with his lessons. I truly don't know if my uncle understood all that had occurred up until this time of him showing up in my life. My frustration boiled over, leading to a moment where I yelled and lashed out, much to his disappointment. My mother disciplined me, and my uncle quietly walked out. That day marked a shift in our relationship. It caused me to reflect deeply on the family dynamics of my mother's side. By this time, I already knew a lot about my father's side of the family through my grandmother, who had been around and supportive in so many ways.

At the age of 14, I was starting to learn the differences between my mother's side of the family and my father's. Interestingly, both my maternal and paternal grandmothers each had four children, but their relationships and dynamics were starkly different. My maternal grandmother, a very fashionable and articulate woman, often visited our home, bringing with her an air of elegance and style.

During one visit, my mother was expressing her frustrations about not having a car to get around for work and daily errands. I believe the dynamic between my sister and my mother, which had become increasingly strained, really made my mother realize that she needed a car to get home sooner. She wanted to start doing more *"motherly"* things with us that were difficult to manage when she was getting home so late. My grandmother (my mother's mother), sensing my mother's struggles, generously gifted her an old Toyota she had recently replaced with a fabulous new truck that perfectly matched her stylish persona. This act of generosity, however, caused friction among the siblings, particularly with my uncle. After my mother received the car, we saw less of him at our house, though my sister and I still kept in contact with him through phone calls and text messages.

Meanwhile, my time at Hamilton Middle School was still marred by bullying, but amidst this darkness, an unexpected bond formed. There was a janitor at the school who took a particular interest in my well-being. It was said that he wanted to protect me from the male students who relentlessly bullied, harassed, and threatened me daily. One day, after school, I was walking home when about ten boys followed me, clearly intent on doing harm. Out of nowhere, this janitor came speeding down the street in his blue car, stopping them before they could lay a hand on me. In that moment, he became more than just a janitor—he became a protector, almost like a big brother or mentor. Our relationship grew stronger throughout my last year, and I began to look up to him for guidance and protection. He was there for me in ways that no one else was, helping me navigate the challenges of middle school. When it came time for my graduation, I remember him meeting my mother and family. My mother thanked him sincerely for the protection and support he had provided me during those difficult years at Hamilton. His presence during that time was a source of comfort, and I'll never forget the impact he had on my life.

As 2000 drew to a close, I stood on the brink of a new chapter, ready to leave middle school behind and step into the unknown world of high school. It was a year that reinforced the importance of family, both biological and chosen, and the unexpected connections that can arise in the most challenging of circumstances. Despite the difficulties and the changes within my family, including my sister no longer living with us, I learned that support can come from the most unexpected places, and that even in times of tension and separation, there is always a path forward.

The Transition Unveiled & The Blessing Embraced

The transitions in 2000 were numerous—moving from middle school to high school, navigating family dynamics with my sister leaving home, and building unexpected bonds with a school janitor who became a protector. The blessing in all this was learning that even in the midst of change and separation, support and resilience can come from unexpected places.

Journal Entry

2001

High school began at a time when I was still navigating the turbulence of my teenage years. I had just turned 15, standing at the precipice of adolescence, carrying the weight of a past that made the future feel uncertain. Looking back, reaching my eighth-grade graduation felt like an improbable victory, but the excitement of leaving middle school was clouded by a deep-seated dread. The memories of the bullying and mistreatment I endured during those years remained vivid, haunting the prospect of what high school might hold for me.

As the year 2001 arrived, the anxiety of stepping into a new environment grew stronger. With the summer of 2000 coming to a close, I knew I needed guidance in finding a high school within my district. My brother was attending Northern High School at the time, and I thought attending the same school might offer some sense of protection. Northern High was on my district's list, and my brother had a network of friends already there. I hoped that being his sibling would shield me from the harshness that high school often brought.

My brother supported my decision and helped me apply to Northern High School. During this period, I spent a lot of time at my grandmother's house, where he was also living. Although he was my half-brother—our connection being through our father rather than our mother—the bond between us grew stronger as he helped me prepare for this new chapter. I admired him greatly, and being close to him provided a sense of security that I desperately needed.

When the school year began, my brother took me under his wing, introducing me to his friends and showing me around the school. As a senior, he was well-established, while I was just starting my journey as a freshman. But soon, things took a sharp turn. His friends would make undertone remarks, saying, *"Oh, your brother is gay. Why didn't you tell us you had a gay brother?"* In 2001, society wasn't as open-minded about homosexuality as it is today. Being gay often meant living in the shadows, in fear of rejection or worse. The world was far from progressive, and openly embracing one's true identity could be dangerous. I found myself questioning why my sexuality was even an issue for them. Why did it matter? This realization made me believe that I needed to change who I was. I tried altering my appearance, adopting the mannerisms of the heterosexual men around me, attempting to fit into a mold that was never meant for me. But no matter how hard I tried, I couldn't suppress my true self. The strain of pretending only deepened my sense of isolation.

Not long after, my brother began to distance himself from me. About a month into the school year, he turned to me one morning as we were on our way to school and said, *"You're a big boy. You go to class on your own."* The protection I had hoped for was suddenly gone. Without his support, I had to navigate the high school environment alone. I was flamboyant, and although I didn't fully understand my sexuality at the time, I knew I was different. Fifteen is a tough age, a crossroads where one grapples with identity, teetering between paths that are unclear and uncertain. Without the support and guidance needed during this critical period, finding the right direction can feel impossible. For me, being 'different' meant feeling like I was standing at a crossroads, with no clear sign of which way to go.

Although I was keenly aware of my difference, beginning my journey at Northern High School also brought new experiences. I began to attract the attention of guys who were interested in me. But having never dated before, I was unsure of how to approach these new interactions. The rules seemed unspoken yet rigid, especially within the African-American community. I recall entertaining the idea of dating a particular guy who quickly asked, "Are you a top or a bottom? You must be a bottom because you're extremely feminine." I equated this to the same hurt I had felt before. Here we were again, back to the issue of femininity. We ended up in a heated argument. I was frustrated that he presumed to know me based on a stereotype and even more so that this was the first topic of conversation when trying to get to know me. That experience left a mark on me, cementing the idea that I didn't want to explore the dating pool further, at least not then.

One incident stands out vividly in my memory. My brother was sick one day, so my grandmother drove me to school alone. I prayed, as I always did before entering the school, holding on to the faith my mother had instilled in me from a young age. But despite my prayers, that day turned into one of the hardest of my life. After two hours of classes, as I was moving from one to the next, three boys jumped me. They beat me so badly that all I could do was curl up in the fetal position on the floor and take the beating. As they hit me, they taunted me, calling me *"gay"* over and over again. When I came to myself and realized the assault was over, I remember the female students rushing over to my side. They always came to my rescue. They helped me up, asking if I was okay, and guided me to clean myself up. It was then that they revealed the identities of my attackers. My heart sank when I learned that the very guy I had been considering dating was among them. This betrayal cut deeply, reinforcing my disdain for dating within the African-American community. It always seemed that the harshest judgments about my femininity and sexuality came from my own people, leaving me confused and hurt as to why my community inflicted the most damage on me.

During lunch that day, I sat alone and prayed again, telling God that I couldn't endure another beating. The fear and pain were too much to bear. I made a decision that day—I would never go back to school. For the remainder of the year, I didn't attend a single class. Instead, I went to my best friend's house, who lived nearby. I'd call her in tears, telling her about the beatings, and she'd comfort me, saying, *"Come over, let's skip school. I'll protect you, and you can stay here."*

Every time my mother asked how school was going, I lied and said everything was fine. But the truth was, I hadn't set foot in Northern High since that day. I spent the rest of my ninth-grade year hiding, trying to survive in a world that felt hostile and unforgiving.

The Transition Unveiled & The Blessing Embraced

The transition in 2001 was the painful move from middle school to high school, marked by a deep sense of fear and the loss of the protection I had hoped for. The blessing, though hard to recognize at the time, was the realization of my inner strength and the importance of self-preservation, even when the world seemed determined to break me down.

Journal Entry

2002

The year 2002 was a pivotal one for me. At 16 years old, I found myself at a crossroads, realizing that I needed to take charge of my life in ways I hadn't before. My sister had moved to Tennessee, leaving just me, my mother, and her *new* boyfriend in our beautiful home. But that house, which should have been a sanctuary, became a place of tension and fear.

My mother's new boyfriend was not only verbally abusive but also physically violent toward her. The abuse filled our home with unbearable tension, and it became clear that he was uncomfortable with my sexuality. His attempts to assert himself as a father figure were met with resistance from me, which only seemed to fuel his frustration even more. As his anger grew, so did the abuse, not just toward my mother but indirectly toward me as well. There was no way that I would endure being abused and made fun of at school and then have to come home to face the same in our beautiful house that my mother worked so hard to secure.

I couldn't stand being in that environment, and I desperately wanted to escape. Not only was I looking to get away from the turmoil at home, but I was also eager to keep myself busy. In the state of Maryland, 16 is the legal age where you can officially start working, and I took full advantage of this. I obtained a work permit and began working at Lee's Ice Cream in downtown Baltimore at the Inner Harbor. The Inner Harbor was an elegant, bustling tourist attraction, situated right on the water, drawing people from all over. I was overjoyed to work there; it was my first time being in an environment filled with people from different walks of life, beyond just schoolmates and family. However, my mother wasn't thrilled about this new job. Since I could only work on weekends—Saturday and Sunday—it meant missing church, especially now that we had started attending a new church. This was a point of contention, as she believed attending church was more important than anything else. So, needless to say, my employment with Lee's Ice Cream Shop didn't last long.

Around this time, things took an even darker turn at home. I vividly remember my mother calling me, her voice trembling as she asked me to come home immediately. Her boyfriend had stolen our furniture and all of the flat-screen TVs that she had worked so hard to provide. That was the breaking point. I knew at that moment that I could no longer tolerate such disrespect, nor could I stand to witness this blatant disregard for my mother any longer. She loved this man, but at this point in my life, I was grasping that love doesn't hurt. Love shouldn't hurt. Love doesn't abuse, and love definitely doesn't steal.

My grandmother's house (my father's mother), which had always been a place of refuge, became even more important to me. I wanted to stay with her permanently, but my mother became resentful of that. She wanted me to protect her from the abuse, but I felt powerless to help. Despite her feelings, my grandmother, with her open arms and understanding heart, allowed me to stay with her as often as my mother would permit.

During my time at my grandmother's, I became close to many family members on my father's side. One of them would become particularly important to me—my dear cousin Sierra Watties, to whom this memoir is dedicated. Sierra and I quickly grew close, and I found myself sharing with her all the pain and devastation of the past years. She listened as I told her about the challenges I faced, including my struggles in school and my dread of returning to high school for my sophomore year after missing most of ninth grade.

Sierra, in her caring and insightful way, suggested that I try attending a youth theater camp she was involved with. She described it as a place filled with gifted, creative people from around Baltimore, and for the first time in a long while, I felt a glimmer of hope. I had always been surrounded by people who didn't accept me for who I was, so the idea of a camp where others like me could express themselves sounded almost too good to be true.

But there was a catch—I didn't know how I would afford it. My mother was barely making ends meet, especially with the financial demands of a new car. I shared this concern with my grandmother, telling her about the camp and how much I thought it could help me. Without hesitation, she offered to pay for the camp as a gift for my 16th birthday. Her generosity opened the door to a new world for me.

I attended the *Arena Players Youth Theater Camp*, and from the moment I walked in, I felt like I had found my tribe. Tears filled my eyes as I took in the scene around me: people expressing themselves freely, singing in the hallways, dancing, and embracing their creativity with a joy I hadn't seen in years. It felt like home in a way I hadn't experienced since my father was alive. My cousin Sierra arrived at the camp later that day, and I thanked her profusely for introducing me to this place. I met so many wonderful people from diverse backgrounds, and though there were cliques and groups, (typical of any group of 16-year-olds), I was eager to know everyone. I found a way to integrate myself into the various groups, driven by a desire to belong.

It was also at Arena Players that I learned that my sexuality was not a barrier here. Kids openly discussed their identities, some even identifying as gay at just 16. For the first time, I saw heterosexual and homosexual boys hanging out together without judgment or malice. It was a liberating environment, one where creativity flourished beyond the restrictive norms that society had imposed. This camp was a glimpse into a world that could accept me for who I was. I started to explore my own identity more boldly— wearing crop tops, ripped jeans, tight jeans, and even started piercing my ears. One day, I stepped out on a limb by asking my mother if I could dye my hair red. To my surprise, she agreed and took me to the salon to get it done. In that moment of my hair being red, I felt a significant milestone—a symbol of her acceptance and a step toward embracing my true self.

Arena Players introduced me to the Baltimore School for the Arts, a prestigious institution nurturing creative talent. The camp was filled with students from this school, and they encouraged me to audition. The idea was daunting— as I had missed so much school, and my self-esteem was hanging by a thread. But I knew I needed something different, something transformative. So, I gave it go and the audition day arrived, my mother couldn't attend due to her work obligation. But, true to her role as my steadfast supporter, my grandmother stepped in and drove me to the school. Her presence was a source of strength in a moment where I was riddled with fear and excitement.

The school itself was magnificent, its aura almost otherworldly. As I stood in the audition room, nerves overtook me. Before I even sang, tears filled my eyes. One of the judges asked what was wrong, and I simply said, *"I'm just so happy to be here."* I sang with all the emotion I could muster, channeling every bit of hope and pain into those songs. Afterward, I called everyone who mattered—my mother, Sierra, my grandmother, even the janitor from Hamilton Middle School, who had been like a big brother to me. I needed them to know I had taken that enormous leap.

A month later, during rehearsals for our production of *The Lion King* at Arena Players, I received an alert from my mother to call her immediately. My heart raced as I thought something tragic had happened, given the abusive situation at home. I rushed to call her from the theater's phone, and when she answered, she told me something that changed everything: I had been accepted to the Baltimore School for the Arts for the 2002 school year.

Life changed dramatically after I received that acceptance letter. I was now a 10th-grade student at the Baltimore School for the Arts, a place that seemed almost mythical to me before I walked through its doors.

The kids I had met at Arena Players, who had now become my friends, were already accustomed to the routine—arriving at school at 8:30 AM and not leaving until 4:30 PM. This was unlike any other city public school, where the focus was solely on academics. At Baltimore School for the Arts, the day was split between honing your craft and completing your academic studies, making the school day much longer.

After school, my friends and I, a tight-knit group from Arena Players, would walk the five blocks to the theater, arriving just in time for our 5:00 PM rehearsals. These rehearsals, lasting from 5:00 PM to 8:00 PM, were some of the most intense three hours I had ever experienced, but they were also incredibly rewarding. Little did I know that these rigorous rehearsals were preparing me for life lessons I would carry with me for years to come.

My first year at Baltimore School for the Arts was one of the hardest experiences of my life. The school was filled with people from all walks of life—many of whom I never even knew lived in Baltimore. It was a melting pot of diversity, with students from various ethnicities, socioeconomic backgrounds, and levels of privilege. I was surrounded by kids who drove Mercedes-Benz and BMWs, wore the latest fashions, and lived in neighborhoods I had only heard about. I was trying to absorb all of this at the age of 16 while balancing the demands of school and the script for *The Lion King* at Arena Players.

I remember struggling with the script, not knowing how to pronounce certain words or even read some of them. It was humiliating, but I was determined not to let these two beautiful opportunities—Arena Players and Baltimore School for the Arts—slip away. I would stay up late into the night, calling friends and asking them not to laugh at me as I sought their help in reading and understanding my lines. Despite the embarrassment, I pushed through, knowing that this was my turning point.

The students at the Baltimore School for the Arts taught me more than just art. They shared knowledge from their households that I had never been exposed to—discussions about personal credit, credit cards, car loans, and financial literacy. These conversations were eye-opening, teaching me life skills that weren't happening at home. I am forever grateful for these kinds of conversations because they opened my eyes to a world that went beyond what I was experiencing on stage and at home.

2002, at age 16, was definitely a year that changed everything for me.

The Transition Unveiled & The Blessing Embraced

The transition in 2002 was moving from a place of fear and uncertainty to discovering a community where I could truly belong. The blessing was the new world of creativity, acceptance, and expression that opened up to me, thanks to the support of my grandmother and the introduction by my cousin Sierra. It was a year that set the stage for the next chapter of my life, filled with hope, new beginnings, and the realization that there was a world where I could be my true self without fear.

Journal Entry

2003

Seventeen found me in a whirlwind, submerged in the relentless demands of my second year at the Baltimore School for the Arts. Each day, the stakes seemed to rise, pulling me deeper into a life where every moment was a delicate balance of dedication and survival.

Days were consumed by the rigorous expectations of one of the city's most prestigious schools. Evenings found me at the Arena Players, not merely performing but delving into a completely different realm of artistic expression. It was here, in the dimly lit theater and amongst a diverse ensemble of artists, that I experienced the raw, unfiltered process of creation.

At the School for the Arts, I was in the throes of becoming a vocal performer, training in the complexities of opera. My baritone voice was shaped and molded through hours of practice, learning new material that ranged from Mozart to Renaissance music. The foreignness of this world was both thrilling and terrifying. Under the guidance of some of the finest instructors, I was inundated with a new language of music theory, diction, and classical techniques. The weight of this knowledge often left me overwhelmed, struggling to keep pace with the rapid flow of learning that engulfed me.

Meanwhile, the Arena Players was a space where I could breathe life into the music I was learning, turning notes into narratives and movements into messages. Here, I learned to merge sound with motion, to block a stage and embody a character fully. It was liberating yet equally demanding. Every rehearsal was three hours of pouring our hearts into the art, pushing ourselves to the very edge of our creative abilities.

There were days I didn't know how I would make it through. The exhaustion was deep and pervasive, yet in those moments, there was no other place I'd rather be than at the Arena Players. It was my refuge, a world apart from the turmoil at home. I longed for things to change, for my mother to wake up and realize that she deserved so much more than the life she was settling for. But until that day came, the theater was my sanctuary, a place where I could escape, even if just for a few hours.

Friendships at the School for the Arts blossomed naturally amidst the shared pressures and joys of artistic pursuit. One friendship, in particular, would become the most enduring—my bond with Sam. Sam and I connected deeply, not just as classmates but as individuals navigating our own turbulent lives. She was wrestling with her own struggles and confided in me about her relationship. In our shared vulnerability, we found strength and became inseparable. Our friendship, forged in those conversations, remains one of the most significant connections in my life.

Outside of school, Baltimore was opening up to me in ways I hadn't expected. I was performing in various music groups that had formed independently of the School for the Arts. Being part of three different groups at once, my musical repertoire was expanding rapidly. It was exhilarating, but also a bit exhausting because of the constant performances and rehearsals that were taking place all at once. Around this time, my sister moved back into our home from

Tennessee, adding another layer of complexity to
my already chaotic life.

I often found myself wondering how my sister and mother
reconnected. What words were exchanged? What healing or
unspoken apologies occurred between them? Yet, in the midst of my
own whirlwind, I never found the time or perhaps the courage to ask
those questions. Their story remained a mystery that lingered in the
background of my daily life, an unresolved thread in the fabric of our
family dynamics.

The fatigue I was starting to experience was profound. My
grandmother was always there, either picking me up from Arena
Players or taking me to her house after picking me up from school.
She became increasingly aware of how worn out I was. I vividly
remember, one day a call came in from the School for the Arts,
informing her that I had been falling asleep in class. It didn't take her
long to understand why. My nights were filled with the sounds of
arguments and fights between my mother and her boyfriend. I stayed
up, ever vigilant, feeling the need to protect her. Yet, I also had to rise
early each morning to face the day ahead. There was no room for
rest.

Desperate for guidance, I sought out the wisdom and comfort that my
mother, (caught in her struggles), couldn't provide. So, I reached out
to those whom I knew would understand and be there in such a time
like this. One of those people being the janitor from Hamilton Middle
School, a man who had been like a big brother and mentor to me in
my earlier years.

He had been trying to connect with me for some time, offering to take
me out to celebrate my achievements. During the reach out via
phone, I poured out my heart, explaining the pressures and demands
that had left me with little time for anything else. During that call, he
suggested we go to my favorite seafood spot on Harford Road, and I
agreed, thinking it might provide a brief escape from my hectic life.

He picked me up from my mother's house and took me to dinner, where I spoke openly about the exhaustion and the need for some sense of normalcy. Afterward, he mentioned the recent renovations at Hamilton Middle School and asked if I wanted to see the changes. I agreed, hoping to revisit the place that had shaped a part of who I was.

As we walked through the school, it quickly became apparent that not much had changed. He led me to his office near the cafeteria—a place filled with memories, both painful and formative. Sitting there, I felt a rush of the past come over me. Then, something happened that I could never have anticipated. His breath lingered on my ear as he whispered, *"I was waiting for you to leave Hamilton, because I've always had a crush on you."* In the same instant, he went in for an unsolicited kiss and grabbed my penis and attempted to hold on to it inappropriately. For those five seconds, it felt like my heart froze. He shattered every bit of trust I had placed in him. I was paralyzed, caught in a whirlwind of emotions, fighting the instinct to flee but trapped by the need to get home safely.

When he dropped me off at my mother's house, I pretended as though nothing had happened when my mother asked what was wrong. Deep down, I knew my mother could sense I was not myself in that moment. Upstairs in my room, I turned on the gospel music that always gave me peace, hoping it would drown out the chaos swirling in my mind. As the familiar melodies filled the space, I found myself wrestling with the grim realization that this was the second time an older African-American man, who claimed to want to help me, had turned out to have other intentions. Why is this a pattern? Is this normal? How many other young African-American boys were enduring similar experiences, left to question their reality in silence? What do I do? Do I simply sweep this under the rug as I saw from other family members that experienced trauma? Or is there a way to process this pain? I had so many questions. But, in the interim, I guess I'll add it to the pile of traumas I was already carrying.

2003 was a year of exhaustion, change, and silent suffering—a year where I learned the harsh reality that even those we trust the most, can betray us. In the end, I found solace not in the external world but within myself, finding small pockets of peace to navigate the deep emotional turmoil.

The Transition Unveiled & The Blessing Embraced

The transition in 2003 was moving from a place of innocence and trust to the harsh reality of betrayal and the need for self-reliance. The blessing was the strength I found within myself to keep going, even when those I looked up to failed me. It was a year that tested my resilience and taught me the importance of finding peace within, even amidst deep emotional turmoil.

Journal Entry

2004

The year 2004 marked a significant turning point in my life. At 18 years old, I was standing at the precipice of adulthood, trying to navigate the final year of my time at the Baltimore School for the Arts, while balancing two jobs and the demands of Arena Players. My plate was full, and I felt the weight of the world on my shoulders. My mother was also in the midst of her own transition; she had recently switched jobs. Having left Bank of America, she was now working in the medical field at a hospital. This new position brought her closer to home, offering a semblance of stability in our lives, yet it also meant that more responsibility fell on my shoulders.

As the year began, I was filled with a mix of anxiety and determination. I knew that this was my last year at Baltimore School for the Arts—a place that had transformed me in so many ways. But as much as I loved the school, I couldn't shake the feeling of pressure building within me. I was still working two jobs: one at Gap, where I had been for two years, and another at Aldo Shoes, where I had been for a year. My mother, struggling with her own challenges, couldn't provide any extra financial support, so I took on these jobs to help myself. I needed more cash flow to cover my own growing expenses, and at this point in my life, there were costs that I had to start managing on my own.

In the midst of all this, a dark and complicated situation continued to loom over me. The janitor from Hamilton Middle School, who had molested and backstabbed me when I was just 17 in 2003, had the audacity to reach out to me as if nothing had happened. His actions left me shattered. When he called, I remember picking up the phone, my mind racing with questions. *"Why? Why? Why?"* I kept asking. His response chilled me: *"Well, you're 18 now, so it doesn't matter."* There was no remorse, no apology for his wrongdoings. That moment changed my perception of people and made me realize just how evil someone could be. I was left feeling confused and trapped, trying to understand what to do about this person who had so callously violated my trust and whom I now desperately wanted out of my life.

As 2004 progressed, one day at Arena Players, I noticed my friends, who had now become like family, were stressed and preparing for something I hadn't even heard of—the SATs. When I asked them what they were, they looked at me in disbelief. I felt embarrassed and out of place, realizing that this critical step toward college had completely passed me by. Not-to-mention, SATs were never echoed in my home.

With anxiety now taking charge, I completed intense research, only to find out that they were already on their second round of SATs, while I hadn't even begun.

Panicking, I turned to my grandmother for help, and she encouraged me to enroll in the next available SAT testing session. Despite my efforts, I failed the first round of SATs. The disappointment was crushing, but deep down, I wasn't entirely surprised. I knew my educational background had been shaky, especially before attending Baltimore School for the Arts. I kept this failure a secret, not wanting to face the embarrassment of my friends, who had all passed their SAT exams. When they asked about my results, I lied, telling them I hadn't taken the test yet.

As my friends prepared to go off to college, I was left without a plan. The realization that I might be left behind was devastating. I started asking around, trying to find any college options that might still be available to me, but everyone I spoke to suggested that community college was my only option. My high school advisors explained that there was nothing else available because I hadn't even known to start the preparation in my junior year. With everything that was going on and no one in my immediate family having gone off to college, I was lost without even realizing it. They told me that no regular college would accept me and that my best option would be to attend community college for a year and then begin applying to other colleges. The idea of attending a community college brought back memories of past traumas. It meant staying in Baltimore, which brought with it the thought of the people and the environment I had already experienced. I was on such a different path at that point in my life and wasn't ready to relive those memories.

In my desperation, I reached out to my uncle, (the educator) within my immediate family, hoping for some guidance or support. Instead, I was met with cold indifference. He reminded me of the time he had tried to help me with Hooked on Phonics and how I had rejected his help. *"That's why you failed,"* he said. *"There's nothing I can do for you now."* His words cut deep, leaving me feeling even more isolated.

Despite everything, I knew I couldn't give up. So, I spoke with the Director of Arena Players, who had become both a mentor and my godfather. I thanked him for everything he had taught me, knowing that my time at Arena Players was coming to an end as well, since they didn't accept members over the age of 18. He had shown me a world beyond Baltimore, taking me on the road with a well-known jazz singer to various concerts, where I witnessed the magic of live performance on a grand scale. Those experiences were invaluable, and I knew they were his way of telling me that the sky was the limit—that there was more out there for me than I had ever imagined.

My love and respect for my godfather deepened during this time. I remember a specific incident that solidified this bond. After one of our performances at Arena Players, an older African-American man, who was a frequent attendee of our shows, came backstage. He often mingled with the cast, so I knew him by face, but not by name at the time. That night, as I was still removing my stage makeup, he entered the dressing room and closed the door behind him. I was taken aback, but I tried to brush it off, assuming he just wanted to congratulate me in private. However, his intentions became clear when he leaned in and kissed me. He was more than 30 years my senior, and in that moment, I felt an all-too-familiar sense of violation. It was happening again. I was paralyzed, flooded with the fear and helplessness I had felt in the past. Yet, this time, the stakes were even higher because I couldn't risk losing my place at Arena Players—a place that had become my sanctuary. The fear of speaking out was immense. I thought that if I reported him, not only would the theater lose a patron, but I might lose my position there.

I couldn't keep this bottled up forever, though. Eventually, I confided in my godfather. The way he responded would forever change my life. Without questioning or blaming me, he took immediate action. I never saw that man in the audience again. My godfather made sure that I was protected, demonstrating in a profound way what it means to truly stand by someone. Even as I write this memoir, my gratitude toward him is beyond words. He didn't just shield me; he restored a piece of my shattered trust.

But just as one door seemed to close, another opened. There was a woman at the church my mother and I attended who had become close to me. Her daughter was on the administrative board at Morgan State University, a renowned HBCU known for its incredible choir under the leadership of Dr. Nathan Carter. I went to her, explained my situation, and asked if there was anything she could do to help me get into Morgan. To my disappointment, she told me that there wasn't. I was devastated, but my godfather, the Director of Arena Players, stepped in once again. He revealed that he had connections at Morgan State and promised to try to get me an audition. Just when I thought all hope was lost, he came through for me. A month later, I auditioned, and to my amazement, I was accepted into Morgan State University.

Though it wasn't the dream I had envisioned—packing up and going off to college like my friends from Arena Players—it was still an incredible blessing. I questioned God during this time, wondering why my path seemed so different from everyone else's. But I knew that maybe, just maybe, there was a bigger plan for me. As much as it hurt to say goodbye to Baltimore School for the Arts and Arena Players, I had learned that life was full of transitions, and with each ending came a new beginning.

The Transition Unveiled & The Blessing Embraced

The transition in 2004 was one of moving from the familiar into the unknown, marked by the challenges of leaving behind the safety nets of Baltimore School for the Arts and Arena Players. The blessing was the unexpected opportunity to continue my education at Morgan State University, a chance to keep growing, learning, and pursuing my dreams, even when the path was uncertain.

Journal Entry

2005

Nineteen was an age where everything around me felt like it was shifting, pulling me into the depths of unfamiliarity. My closest friends had ventured off to different colleges, leaving me to face the tangled web of adulthood without them close by. It was as if the life I knew had been uprooted, leaving me to navigate a world that was no longer steady or safe. In this whirlwind of change, the one constant was my best friend, Sam. She was more than a friend; she was my anchor, the quiet in the storm that was brewing in every corner of my life.

Although Sam and I were already close, our bond deepened significantly during this period. She was unaware of the abusive relationship my mother had endured with her previous partner, and also unaware that my mother had entered into another relationship that was just as toxic. This new relationship was also fraught with verbal and physical abuse, and at 19, I began to recognize the disturbing patterns that were emerging in my life, my mother's life, and our family history. I started to ask myself mature questions— questions about our childhoods, our choices, and the cycles of pain we seemed destined to repeat. But these were questions I didn't yet have the answers to, so they lingered in the background, unresolved.

It was during this time that I started to see the repetition of domestic violence as a haunting thread woven into the fabric of my family's history. Was my mother seeking something in these relationships, the same thing I was desperately searching for in my own life? While I could recognize my own longing for love and acceptance, I knew that my mother's pattern was not one I wanted to replicate. The clarity of this realization was jarring. It made me question the choices we make and the power we have over our own narratives. My mother had control, at least to some extent, over whether she stayed in these toxic situations. Yet, there was a part of me that understood her choice to stay—it was tied to something much deeper, a legacy of brokenness passed down through generations. The acknowledgment of this family-rooted history was like looking into a mirror that reflected not just my present but also the shadows of our past. It was the beginning of my deeper awareness of the cycles we become entangled in and the silent battles we carry within us.

Sam, with her open-mindedness, spiritual connection to nature, and deep wisdom, often challenged me to think critically about my life and the world around me. She was the one person I could turn to for insight and perspective, and I was grateful to have her so close by. Her house was only six blocks from my mother's, making it easy for me to escape there whenever I needed a break from the chaos at home. The bike rides from my mother's house to Sam's became a form of therapy for me—a time to release the pent-up emotions and anger that had no other outlet.

In addition to the emotional turmoil, I was also dealing with the practical challenges of balancing my new life at Morgan State University with my responsibilities at home. I was still working two jobs—one at Aldo Shoes and another at Gap—while trying to keep up with the demands of college. However, as I became more involved with the Morgan State University choir, which began to travel frequently, I realized I could no longer maintain both jobs. The choir had become a significant part of my life, and I had to make sacrifices to keep up with its demanding schedule.

Because I had given up my jobs, I had more free time, and my mother would often allow me to use her car—the precious red Toyota that my grandmother had gifted her. This car was my mother's pride and joy, a symbol of her independence and resilience. She had cherished it ever since my grandmother had given it to her, and she entrusted me with it when I needed to get to school or run errands.

One day, after dropping my mother off at work, I headed to Morgan State University for my classes. Later, I planned to go to the store with some friends from the university. As we drove, we blasted a new tune we had learned in choir, singing along and enjoying the moment. But in my distraction, I took an unfamiliar road and suddenly found myself in a horrific accident. I crashed into the back of another car so hard that it totaled my mother's beloved red Toyota. The engine was hanging out of the car, and I was in shock. In a state of panic, I drove home, leaving the scene of the accident without fully understanding the consequences of my actions.

As I sat on my mother's porch with my friends, trying to muster the courage to call her and explain what had happened, a black car pulled up. A man got out, pointing a gun at me, and demanded to know why I had left the scene after crashing into his car. It was a moment of sheer terror. I was devastated—not only had I destroyed my mother's most prized possession, but I had also put myself and my friends in danger. I felt an overwhelming sense of guilt, knowing that my actions had brought unnecessary stress and financial burden onto my mother.

When my mother arrived home, she was distraught. She didn't have words for me—just tears. Those tears still haunt me, as I could see the deep pain and worry in her eyes. She had to call on my ever-faithful grandmother to pick her up, and I knew she was wondering how she would manage to work and take care of us without a car, yet again. I offered to stay home to comfort her, but she told me to go on my scheduled trip with the Morgan State University choir, who were set to perform *Porgy and Bess* in Prague, Czech Republic. She said she needed time away from me, and I reluctantly agreed.

The Transition Unveiled & The Blessing Embraced

The transition in 2005 was about moving from a place of dependency and naivety to a deeper awareness of the impact of my actions on others. The blessing was the hard lesson in accountability and the beginning of a journey toward understanding the patterns in my life that needed to change. It was a year that set the stage for future growth and self-discovery.

Journal Entry

2006

By this time, my bond with the Morgan State University Choir was stronger than ever. The choir had become my family, a group of individuals with whom I shared a deep connection. We were traveling all over the world, experiencing new cultures, and performing in places I had only dreamed of. Fresh off the performance in Prague, I was home for only two weeks when I received the news that we were off to Italy next. The excitement of these adventures was intoxicating, and I was meeting people who were opening my eyes to a world far beyond Baltimore, Maryland.

My musical journey wasn't confined to Morgan State alone. By 2006, I had further established myself within the Baltimore music scene, singing not just with the Morgan State Choir but also with other renowned choirs and in various venues across the city. I was performing in churches, at events, and even in local bars, slowly building a name for myself. Music was my life, and it seemed like I was finally beginning to find my place in the world.

It was during one of these trips, this time to Paris, that I met someone who would forever change the course of my life. After our choir performed, I met a Parisian musician at a local bar. There was something about his accent, his wisdom, and his understanding of life that captivated me. We spent the evening talking about our dreams, our passions, and our next steps. When he asked me what I saw for my future, I hesitated. Up until that point, I had only ever imagined singing gospel and opera—genres that had shaped my musical foundation. But this man, with his deep understanding of music, suggested something different.

"There's a school you should consider," he said. *"It's in Boston, Massachusetts—a renowned jazz school that people from all over the world, especially in Europe, dream of attending. You should look into it."* The school he was referring to was Berklee College of Music. I had never heard of it, despite being an American, and the fact that he spoke so highly of it intrigued me. As he shared more about Berklee, I realized he wasn't just talking about a school; he was showing me a new path, a different way of thinking about my future.

Tears welled up in my eyes as I began to understand what life was truly about—connection, being present in the moment, and listening to the voices that guide us. This man, whom I had only just met, felt like a messenger from God, pointing me toward a new direction. Though our time together in Paris was brief, it left a lasting impression on me.

When I returned to the States, I immediately began researching Berklee College of Music, my mind swirling with all the things that the stranger—whom I now knew to be a gift from God—had tried to explain to me. I felt an unshakable pull to uncover more, to see for myself what was possible. As I dove deeper into my research, I discovered something that felt like divine intervention: Berklee conducted traveling auditions. When I saw that they were coming to Baltimore, Maryland, it felt like God's way of nudging me forward, confirming that this was a path I needed to take.

Summoning every ounce of courage I had, I navigated their website and scheduled myself for an audition. I told no one—not my mother, not my closest friends. This dream was tender and new, and I felt I needed to protect it until I knew it could stand on its own.

As I was preparing for my audition, which was to be held at the Eubie Blake Jazz Center in downtown Baltimore, I received a text from my best friend, Sam. She asked me to meet her at Starbucks, and as always, I dropped everything to be by her side. When I arrived, Sam shared some news that left me devastated—she had been accepted to the college of her choice and would be leaving Baltimore. Sam was the last person from my familiar world, and knowing she was about to leave left me feeling even more alone.

In the face of this loss, I channeled my emotions into preparing for my Berklee audition. A month later, I auditioned, and to my amazement, I was accepted. When the acceptance letter arrived in the mail—back when letters still held such power—I was overwhelmed with emotion. Seeing the Berklee College of Music logo on the envelope, I knew my life was about to change. I was either going to be ecstatic or heartbroken depending on what the rest of the letter said. When I read the words *"Congratulations, Jordan. You have been accepted to Berklee College of Music in Boston,"* I felt a rush of excitement and disbelief.

I couldn't wait to share the news with my mother, so I called her at work. But to my surprise, her response wasn't what I had hoped for. Instead of sharing in my joy, she told me, *"I don't want you to go. Let's discuss it when I get home."* Her words shattered me. I had expected her to be overjoyed, to scream with excitement, but instead, I was met with hesitation. Why wasn't she excited for me? Was she still angry about the car I had totaled? Did she fear losing me, or was it because of the child support check incident that changed our relationship?

For as long as I could remember, my mother had received a child support check from my father. My grandmother—his mother—made sure it arrived every month without fail. At some point, the checks started coming in the mail— in my name, though my mother continued to use them. I never questioned it as I understood how much she had sacrificed to provide for me and how deeply she cared.

However, she had once told me that when I turned 18, the checks would be mine entirely. There would be no deductions, no percentages kept. This agreement stuck with me, and when I turned 18, I anticipated a transition where I would take responsibility for these funds.

Then the day came. The check arrived in the mail, and I took it. I told her I planned to cash it, just as we had agreed. But instead of support, I was met with resistance. I vividly remember her snatching the check from my hand and telling me that, unfortunately, our agreement had to change—she needed the money.

What followed was a painful moment. Emotions ran high. She pushed me as she tried to take the check, and I pushed her back in an effort to keep it. It was a horrible, heartbreaking exchange, one that still weighs heavily on me. Money should never come between a mother and son, yet there we were, caught in a struggle that felt bigger than both of us.

Looking back now, I see it differently. I was transitioning into adulthood, preparing for college, and there was so much I needed. If only we had sat down and talked—if only she had explained what she was going through—maybe I could have offered her a percentage, 5 or 10%, to help with whatever she needed. Maybe we could have worked together instead of against each other.

It was a difficult time for both of us, one that made me see my mother in a different light. Writing about this now, I realize how much we both were carrying—her as a mother who had given so much and still needed more, and me as an 18-year-old trying to navigate independence. It wasn't just about the check. It was about the unspoken struggles we were both facing, and the way we missed an opportunity to understand one another.

So many questions raced through my mind during this time, but I didn't want to face them— not in that moment. All I wanted was to bask in the moment of my Berklee acceptance. But I knew, even at 20, that I needed her support. There were forms to fill out, paperwork to sign—things I couldn't do on my own. More than that, I needed her to be excited for me, to believe in this next chapter of my life as much as I did.

The Transition Unveiled & The Blessing Embraced

The transition in 2006 was about moving from a place of familiarity and safety to embracing the unknown. The blessing was the courage to pursue a new path, to believe in the possibility of something greater, even when the people I loved were hesitant. It was a year that taught me the importance of following my heart and trusting in the journey, no matter how uncertain it might seem.

Journal Entry

2007

Accepted into one of the most prestigious music schools in the world, Berklee College of Music in Boston, I found myself on the brink of a new chapter. This was a reality that had once seemed so distant from the life I had known in Baltimore. Preparing for this departure stirred a whirlwind of emotions within me—excitement, fear, and uncertainty. Leaving behind everything familiar was both terrifying and exhilarating.

This journey was set in motion by my dear cousin, Sierra Watties. It all began with a conversation at my grandmother's house that led me to the Arena Players. There, I found a community of like-minded souls who became my chosen family. Through them, I discovered the performing arts and eventually found my way to Baltimore School for the Arts, where my talents were nurtured and refined. My godfather, the Director of Arena Players, opened doors for me at Morgan State, where I was able to travel the world with the university choir. In Paris, I met a man whose wisdom and kindness introduced me to Berklee College of Music—a school I had never heard of but which quickly became my dream.

Despite the overwhelming odds, I knew I had to pursue what the universe had laid before me.

Yet, standing on the brink of this new chapter, I encountered an unexpected and painful obstacle—my mother's indifference. I couldn't understand why she wasn't excited for me or supportive of my transition to Berklee. Was she still angry about the car accident that totaled her car? Was she afraid of losing me, her last child still at home? Questions swirled in my mind, but answers eluded me. All I knew was that I had to face this challenge on my own.

As I relive the day of my audition from 2006, it felt like walking into destiny. The air was thick with both anticipation and possibility, and I could feel the weight of the moment as I stepped inside. This wasn't just another audition—*this was the audition.* A chance to unlock a future I had dreamed about for so long.

I had chosen to open with "His Eye Is on the Sparrow," a gospel tune that had always comforted me in moments of uncertainty. As I sang, I felt the weight of the world lift, replaced by a calm that I knew wasn't mine alone. The room was still, almost reverent, and in those minutes, it felt as though every struggle I'd endured and every hope I carried had found its way into that melody.

My second piece was "Deep River," an operatic spiritual I felt deeply connected to. Its haunting beauty seemed to flow through me, carrying not only my voice but my heart to a place beyond the notes. The judges' faces were a mix of curiosity and awe, and as I finished, I could see them exchanging glances. They didn't say much at first, but their expressions said it all.

"Thank you," one of them said with a nod that felt weighty with meaning. "Please proceed to the next room."

I quickly realized that this audition wasn't just about performance; it was a full-scale evaluation. The process spanned over three hours, testing not just my singing ability but also my stamina, my focus, and perhaps even my resolve. Each step forward felt monumental, as though I was being guided toward something life-changing, something bigger than myself.

After completing the performance portion, I was directed to meet with financial advisors. The transition from the music room to the world of numbers and logistics was jarring, but it was a crucial part of the process. They laid out the costs of tuition, the scholarships available, and the grants I might be eligible for should I be accepted. It wasn't just about being talented enough—it was about ensuring I was equipped to make this dream a reality.

By the time the audition process was over, I was emotionally drained yet exhilarated. For the first time in my life, I could see the possibility of stepping into my purpose and claiming it fully. Berklee felt closer than ever, and in that moment, I knew I had given them everything I had—and then some.

But, they asked the life-changing question: "After hearing everything, do you have any questions?" I immediately explained to them that I didn't come from a family of means and would need financial assistance, sadly. To my surprise, they couldn't offer a scholarship at the time. I was devastated. The prospect of not being able to attend Berklee due to financial constraints felt like a cruel twist of fate. I remember lying across the bed, tears streaming down my face as I grappled with the possibility of this dream slipping away.

With nowhere else to turn, I reached out to my grandmother. *"Grandma, I need you like never before. My mother isn't supporting or encouraging me, and I need to find a way to Berklee."* She had always been a source of strength, making a way out of no way— and I hoped she could do the same now.

Unfortunately, she couldn't help with a loan for the tuition difference, but she offered to rent a car if I could find someone to drive me to Boston. I couldn't even afford a plane ticket.

Determined to make this work, I reached out to everyone I knew— those who had once told me, *"If you ever need anything, reach out to me."* In my desperation, I called, emailed, and texted everyone I had confided in or met along the way this far in life. I contacted my chosen family's parents, people from Morgan State, Arena Players, Baltimore School for the Arts, and even the pastor of the church my mother, sister, and I had attended faithfully for the past three years. Despite the offers of support in the past, when I needed it most, there was no one who could help me make the leap to Boston. The weight of this realization was crushing.

One Sunday after service, I approached the pastor and whispered, *"Pastor, I need your help. Please call or send me an email when you can."* He acknowledged my request, but his response seemed dismissive. That evening, I sent him an email instead explaining my situation. I believed, perhaps naively, that he would respond with enthusiasm. Instead, he replied that he would see what he could do, and mentioned having some grant books he could provide in hopes of one of the grants being approved in time.

After a few email exchanges, we arranged to meet at the church so he could give me the grant books. It was a Tuesday— I arrived at the church and saw his car parked outside, confirming that he was indeed there. As I approached the door, it was unlocked, so I let myself in, expecting to find him in the foyer. When I didn't see him, I texted, *"I see your car is here, but I don't see you. Where are you?"* He replied, asking me to meet him in his office.

As I climbed the stairs of the church, I felt a wave of discomfort. It struck me as odd that we were meeting in his office, but I brushed it aside, reasoning that perhaps that's where the grant books were. When I entered, he was sitting behind his desk, surrounded by the familiar objects of his workspace—a fax machine behind him, a telephone to his right, file cabinets, and pictures of his family scattered around. I sat in the chair opposite his desk, closest to the entrance of the office.

We began discussing Berklee—the cost, the tuition difference—and suddenly, the conversation shifted. He started asking about my personal life: *"Who are you dating? Boys or girls?"* He probed, trying to confirm things about me that I didn't feel comfortable discussing. I was hesitant to answer, but part of me felt compelled to comply. He was my pastor, after all. I had been taught to hold pastors in high regard, to trust them.

It wasn't long before he grabbed the dusty, outdated grant books, clearly unfamiliar with them, and invited me to come around the desk to read them with him. It seemed unnecessary, but I complied, not knowing what he had planned. And then, without my consent and to my shock, he slipped his hand down my pants and fingered my anus; all while quickly going in for a kiss with tongue.

I froze. My body felt numb, my mind racing. Memories of past betrayals surged forward, yet again. I pulled away and told him, "You can't do this." But it was too late—the damage had been done.

I left the church with the grant books in hand, their dust a symbol of the betrayal I had just endured. Driving home, I blasted gospel music, hoping the familiar melodies would drown out the confusion and pain that now weighed heavily on my heart. When I got home, I handed my mother the books, but she was too absorbed in her own anger to ask questions or notice my distress. So, I did what I had always done—I retreated to my room, buried my feelings, and pushed forward. But with this being the fourth devastating betrayal, I knew deep in my soul that something had to change—immediately.

The financial gap standing between me and Berklee College of Music was still unresolved, and now the burden felt even heavier.

Desperate to leave Baltimore, I called my best friend, Sam. *"Sam,"* I said, my voice trembling, *"I know you're in New York right now, but I have to get out of here. Can you say a prayer with me? I want to pray that I never return to this place that has scarred me so deeply."* We prayed, and following it, Sam immediately put me in touch with her sister, someone she knew I could count on and who was located in Baltimore.

At that point, it didn't matter whether I had the means to cover the tuition difference or not—I was leaving, no matter what. My broken and shattered heart couldn't bear to remain in Baltimore any longer. I had no idea what was going to happen or how it would all unfold; I just knew one thing with absolute certainty: I was out.

Leading up to my departure, I stopped going to the church where the pastor had betrayed me. I asked Sam's sister about the church she attended, and she told me it was a place focused on delivering the message without judgment, where the pastor helped people through their hardest times. It sounded like exactly what I needed as I continued to process everything. So, I went with her, seeking peace-of-mind, and at the same time, people from my old church began texting and calling, asking why I had left and where I had been. I made up excuses, not wanting to reveal what their pastor had done to me. I was laser-focused on leaving Baltimore at this point.

My relationship with Sam's sister grew stronger through these days. She had been part of the Morgan State University choir too, but we weren't as close then as we were now. Sam had made the connection between us, and I felt comfortable enough to open up about needing her help to drive me to Boston. With her support, my departure was set.

I planned to leave on September 4th, the day after my mother's birthday. When I told my mother I was leaving, she reacted with anger and resistance. *"You're not leaving,"* she said firmly. But I knew I had to go.

On the morning of September 4th, Sam's sister called me. *"I just picked up the van," she said."* I'll be at your house by 4PM so we can pack up the van." When she arrived, my mother stood there with anger in her eyes. I had so many questions for her, but there was no time for answers or confrontations. As we loaded my belongings into the van, I couldn't help but wonder if I would ever speak to my mother again.

Finally, we pulled away, and I turned on gospel music. After ten long hours on the road, we arrived in Boston, Massachusetts. The city felt like a world apart from Baltimore, but, I was excited to finally arrive.

Once everything was unloaded, I hugged Sam's sister tightly. Her willingness to drive me all the way to Boston meant more to me than she would ever know. I couldn't find the words to fully express my gratitude, but in that embrace, I hoped she felt the depth of my appreciation. She wasn't just helping me move to a new city; she was part of the bridge between my old life and the unknown future ahead.

As we made the last trip upstairs to my dorm room, I sensed the finality of leaving my old life behind. Every step up that staircase felt like I was shedding layers of the past—Baltimore, my family, the struggles I thought I'd escaped. This was a fresh start, but also an uncertain one.

That first night, I waited anxiously for my new roommate to arrive, each minute feeling like an eternity. When he finally did, we introduced ourselves. He was from Texas, and had brought his mother and little brother along to help him settle in. Tears welled up as I realized how different our situations were. While he had the support of his family, surrounding him with warmth and security, I was navigating this new chapter on my own. That stark contrast hit me harder than I expected, reminding me that this journey would test me in ways I hadn't fully prepared for.

Later that night, as I lay in bed with my headphones on, listening to gospel music, I couldn't fully sleep. The familiar melodies should have brought me peace, but instead, my mind raced with the thoughts of unpaid tuition and the new world I was about to enter. The weight of those worries pressed down on me, making the bed feel too big, too cold, and too lonely. The next morning, instead of joining my roommate for breakfast, I rushed to the bursar's office, knowing that the unpaid balance could jeopardize everything. Fear gripped me, but beneath that fear was a determination that I couldn't afford to lose.

The bursar's office offered some options—government loans and student jobs. I applied for the jobs immediately, my hands shaking as I filled out the forms. I reached out to my grandmother once again (thinking her situation might have changed), asking if she could co-sign a loan. But with my aunt now influencing many of her decisions, and with others living in her home after my grandfather's passing, the extra funds she could once provide were no longer available. I even reached out to my uncle *(the "educator")*, hoping he would understand the gravity of my situation. But no one was willing to co-sign, and I was left to face this hurdle alone.

Despite these setbacks, I kept faith. Deep down, I knew that somehow, I had to make this work. I had no other choice. As the semester progressed, I met students from all walks of life. Many were already financially secure, their educations fully paid for. I couldn't help but wonder how they had so much at such a young age while I was struggling just to stay afloat. But I didn't let that envy consume me. Instead, it fueled my determination to keep pushing forward.

My roommate was my first real connection, and though he was kind and accepting of me, he had his own life to live. He had his family, his support system, and his own world to explore. While he ventured out into Boston, I was left to navigate my own path, forced to step out of my comfort zone and meet new people. It was a beautiful thing, though. I learned that loneliness wasn't something to be feared but embraced as a stepping stone to personal growth. I remember Boston being so cold. I know a lot of people think Chicago is cold, but Boston's winter had a bite that cut straight through you.

We would go over the bridge to Harvard University and hang out there, and I met some wonderful people who brought light into my life during a time when darkness often loomed. My favorite spot was a gay club called Club Café, in my opinion, the best gay club in Boston. I don't know why I didn't buy stock—haha—that's how often I was there. My love for techno music started there; we would dance the night away, completely lost in the rhythm and energy of the room. I found a sense of freedom on that dance floor, a place where I could shed the weight of my worries, if only for a few hours. We'd leave that place drenched in sweat, only to walk back to the dorms through the freezing streets, wondering why we were sick in the morning. I can still hear the laughter as we shivered our way back, too full of life to care about the consequences. We had walked home in wet clothes, but those moments were worth it.

Boston also had these beautiful, large parks where everyone would meet up, study, and do homework. It was more than just a place to learn; it was a place to belong. The city itself was alive with the energy of students and dreamers. It felt like everyone around me was at the beginning of their own story, eager to write the next chapter. The food was amazing, and I remember Newbury Street stretching for what seemed like miles, filled with restaurants and beautiful clothing shops. It was a town where everyone was just happy to be away from their families, starting their college life. I could sense that this was a time to build a community, to form bonds that would last a lifetime. For the first time, I truly felt that I had the opportunity to create a life on my own terms, outside of everything that had defined me in childhood.

I settled into life at Berklee College of Music, but the weight of everything I had left behind in Baltimore pressed heavily on me. The excitement of being in a new city was often overshadowed by the reality of how far I was from home—both physically and emotionally. The pace was fast, and I struggled to keep up. Every day was a battle to stay afloat, but each battle felt like a step forward, no matter how small. I spent countless hours in office hours, seeking extra help from my professors, who were understanding but unable to slow down the curriculum for just one student. Hiring a private tutor was suggested, but that was out of the question. Money was tight—tighter than anyone around me knew. The burden of my financial struggles weighed me down, but I carried it in silence, unwilling to let anyone see just how close I was to breaking.

Despite these challenges, I pushed forward. My determination kept me going, even as I cried myself to sleep many nights, wondering if I had made the right choice in coming to Boston. It wasn't just about the education anymore; it was about proving to myself that I could survive, that I could carve out a space in this world, even if the odds were stacked against me.

As the semester came to a close and students began leaving for their homes or vacation spots, I was left with the harsh reality that I had nowhere to go. My family couldn't afford to bring me back to Baltimore, and the dorms required us to vacate for the summer. The weight of uncertainty was crushing, but as I had done so many times before, I kept pushing forward. I told myself that I would find a way, just as I always had.

Then, in a moment of vulnerability, everything changed. After a yoga class, where I had unexpectedly burst into tears, a fellow student approached me with a kind offer. She noticed that I was struggling and offered me a place to stay. She had a spare room in her apartment and, without hesitation, extended her generosity to me. Overwhelmed with gratitude, I accepted. In that moment, I realized that even in the darkest times, there are people willing to help. Sometimes, the most unexpected blessings come when you need them the most. Moving into her apartment felt like a small victory amidst the chaos. It was a chance to catch my breath and gather myself after everything that had happened. The summer brought a brief sense of stability, a respite from the relentless uncertainty that had followed me since leaving Baltimore.

This kindness was a turning point—a reminder that, despite the hardships, there were still good people willing to lend a hand. It wasn't a solution to all my problems, but it was a lifeline when I needed it most. That summer, as I stayed in her apartment, I allowed myself to dream again. I began to believe that maybe, just maybe, things could turn around for me.

The Transition Unveiled & The Blessing Embraced

The transition from Baltimore to Boston was a tumultuous journey filled with unexpected challenges and betrayals. Each step forward seemed to bring new hurdles that tested my resilience. However, this chapter of my life unveiled a strength I never knew I had. It pushed me to confront my fears and insecurities head-on, forcing me to grow in ways I didn't realize I was capable of.

The blessing in this transition lay in the realization that help can come from the most unexpected places. It wasn't the people I had relied on before, nor the ones who had promised to support me. Instead, it was a fellow student—a near stranger—who extended a hand when I felt most alone. This act of kindness taught me that the universe has a way of providing what we need, even when we least expect it. The journey was far from over, but this chapter marked the beginning of my understanding that transitions, though painful, can bring forth the most profound blessings. Sometimes, it's in our lowest moments that we are shown the greatest light.

Journal Entry

2008

In 2008, I was 22 years old, trying to navigate life with the tools I had, though those tools often felt insufficient for the task at hand. I remember vividly moving into the apartment of my newly dear friend, someone I had grown close to through our regular yoga classes. We had met up every other day, sharing our lives and learning from one another. She was pursuing her teacher training certification in yoga, and through this journey, our bond deepened. This wasn't just any apartment; it was a luxurious penthouse on the corner of Mass Ave and Newbury in Boston—a place everyone talked about. Somehow, it became my home too.

The penthouse was like something out of a dream, with floor-to-ceiling windows that offered a breathtaking view of the city below. It had all the trappings of luxury—a doorman, top-tier security, and an air of exclusivity that was almost suffocating. My new roommate warned me that this building was home to some of the most elite and important people in Boston—doctors, mayors, senators—and that we needed to be mindful of that. Despite everything, she trusted me, allowed me into her life, and now, into her home.

By this time, I had completed my second year at Berklee College of Music and was starting to gain recognition in the Boston music scene. I had performed at the prestigious Singer's Night at Berklee—a feat that not many could achieve. My new address at 360 Newbury Street came with a certain allure, and I found myself being invited to places and events that I could have only dreamed of before. I was meeting powerful people—people with influence and connections that could change the trajectory of my life. Yet, despite all the glamour, I was struggling internally. I often found myself leaving the beautiful penthouse to walk over to the student mailboxes, hoping to find care packages or cards from home—something to celebrate the milestone of being the first in my immediate family to go to college. But every time, I was met with emptiness. There was never anything there, and that absence felt like a quiet echo of how disconnected I was becoming.

This year was a pivotal time for me, but also one of the most sensitive periods of my life. With me now knowing my way around Boston, I started to hang out more and attend certain clubs on weekends or whenever I had the time. It was during this period that I got involved with a well-known doctor from a prestigious hospital in Boston. Around the same time, I met a director at Harvard University at an event, and we became very close as well. I remember dating these two men simultaneously, but it was never about getting serious. I already had too much on my plate and was primarily focused on staying enrolled at Berklee College of Music.

As I entered my fifth semester at Berklee, my roommate informed me that she would be leaving Berklee and returning to her home country. She trusted me so much that she left her penthouse in my care, along with her dog, who quickly became my dog. This dog became my lifeline, offering me unconditional love in a world where I often felt lost.

But with this new responsibility came more stress. I was struggling to keep it all together—trying to stay afloat at Berklee while dealing with the reality that my grandmother could no longer support me financially. The pressures of maintaining my place in the penthouse, the demands of my studies, and the burden of my past began to weigh heavily on me. My mind was constantly racing with thoughts about how I would manage to continue my education and what my future would hold.

With nowhere else to turn, I began spending more time with the doctor from the prestigious hospital and the director at Harvard. I was looking to them for advice, trying to see if they knew of any programs or opportunities that could help me stay at Berklee. I opened up to them, allowing myself to be vulnerable. But during this consistent hanging out, they introduced me to an array of substances. We would partake together, and I noticed how these substances started to numb the pain, the fear, the overwhelming sense of inadequacy. The more I used, the more I needed, and soon, my life became a cycle of partying, drugs, and trying to keep up appearances.

The semester ended, and I somehow managed to get through it, but I was barely holding on. I was interning at Click Model Management, working full-time at Kenneth Cole, and trying to make ends meet. But I was falling apart inside. The pressures of maintaining the penthouse, caring for the dog, and dealing with the demands of school were too much. I started to spiral, turning more and more to drugs to numb the pain.

Sam had been calling and texting me for some time to check-in, but I hadn't been answering. She knew this wasn't like me. One day, out of the blue she showed up unannounced at the penthouse. One look at the state I was in, at the chaos that had consumed my life, and she made a decision that would save me. Sam packed up my belongings, gathered up the dog, and rented a U-Haul. She took the same route that her sister had taken two years earlier, driving me back to Baltimore. She stored my things and checked me into a rehab facility, where I stayed for three months without any contact with the outside world. I detoxed, met with therapists and psychologists, and slowly began to confront the demons that had been haunting me. I started to reclaim a sense of self, as I finally allowed myself to process the deep wounds of molestation and the many losses that had occurred.

It was a relief I hadn't known I needed, and for the first time, I understood the weight of my unresolved trauma. I owe that awakening to Sam, who took it upon herself to ensure I sought the help that ultimately saved my life. I hadn't realized the toll such buried pain could take, not just on the body, but on the mind as well. In the African-American community, the concept of therapy and confronting one's emotions is often dismissed, leaving so many to silently endure. But in this moment, I chose not to endure — I chose to heal.

When I finally left rehab on November 28, 2008, I had missed Thanksgiving, but I had gained something far more valuable—I had regained a sense of myself. It wasn't long before Sam made a decision to take me with her to New York City, the place she now called home. She wanted to keep me close, to ensure that I stayed on the right track, because that's how much I meant to her.

The Transition Unveiled & The Blessing Embraced

2008 was a year of intense struggle, where the facade I had built around myself began to crumble. But it was also a year of salvation, where the love and care of a true friend pulled me back from the brink. The transition from the chaos of Boston to the safety of New York City was a painful one, but it was necessary. In embracing this transition, I began to understand the power of letting go—of releasing the things that no longer served me and allowing space for healing and growth. The blessing was in the return to myself, in finding strength in the love of those who truly cared for me, and in beginning the journey of healing that would shape the next chapter of my life.

Journal Entry

2009

In 2009, at 23 years old, I found myself in a new chapter of life, feeling refreshed and more aligned with my identity, especially with my homosexuality. Therapy had taught me so many valuable lessons—namely, to acknowledge my past, feel it deeply, address the issues, and then let them go. This year was about embracing the person I was becoming and navigating life with more confidence and self-awareness.

Sam and I had settled into Spanish Harlem, on 151st Street and Broadway. The neighborhood was alive with the vibrancy of the Latino culture—an experience completely different from anything I had known before. Moving to New York City was a massive change, and while I was somewhat familiar with its reputation as *"The Big Apple,"* living there was a different story altogether.

Our apartment was small, almost claustrophobic, and it was a far cry from the spacious places I had lived in before. Everything in the building was controlled—whether it was the heat regulated by the building's management or the view from the window, which was simply another apartment just feet away. I quickly learned that to fit in, I needed to adapt to my surroundings, including learning some basic Spanish greetings to navigate life in Spanish Harlem. It wasn't just about language; it was about respect and survival in an area where I was a newcomer.

The building, as I later learned, had a reputation of its own. It was known for its connections to the drug trade and possibly even the mafia. The landlord, who seemed to command a certain respect or even fear from the tenants, reinforced this suspicion. I kept my head down, following Sam's advice to stay inside as much as possible during the first three months. My outings were limited to walking the dog down to the Hudson River, where I found a bit of peace and space in an otherwise confined life.

Despite the challenges, I began to feel the pull to work again. I've always been someone who needed a plan, and after two months of settling in, I started reaching out to my contacts in Boston. The connections I had made there paid off, and soon enough, I had secured an internship at Click Model Management in New York, along with a full-time job at Kenneth Cole on Fifth Avenue. I was eager to share the news with Sam, but I was also aware that she might have something to share as well.

When the three-month mark hit, Sam sat me down and told me that she had fallen in love and would be moving back to Baltimore. Although I had a feeling this was coming, it still stung. She had been my rock, the one who helped me restart my life, but I understood that it was time for both of us to move on.

With her departure, she took our beloved dog with her—a decision that was difficult but necessary given my new circumstances. Sam found a beautiful new place for me on 130th Street, closer to the cultural heartbeat of Harlem, near the Apollo Theater. This area was steeped in Black culture, something I had always dreamed of being a part of. So, with a mix of sadness and hope, I said goodbye to Sam as she returned to Baltimore. I was left to navigate my new life in New York, interning at Click Model Management and working full-time at

Kenneth Cole. It was a new beginning in many ways, and although I was scared, I knew this was where I needed to be.

The Transition Unveiled & The Blessing Embraced

In 2009, I discovered that new beginnings often come with unexpected farewells. Embracing my identity and facing the realities of life in a new city pushed me to grow in ways I hadn't anticipated. The strength to adapt, learn, and move forward came from within, guided by the love and support of those who had been there when I needed them most. This chapter taught me that even when the path is uncertain, taking the first step is what leads to transformation.

Journal Entry

2010

2010 was a year of unexpected turns. At 24, my life was in flux, a balance between ambition and the unknown. The hustle of New York City had become my backdrop, a place where every decision felt like a step into uncharted territory. My best friend had moved on, leaving me to navigate this vast city alone. In this solitude, I discovered a new kind of strength, one that demanded I face what lay ahead with resolve.

Working full-time at Kenneth Cole was demanding, and while my internship at the modeling agency was providing invaluable lessons, I just couldn't keep balancing it all. I remember the early mornings, leaving my small Harlem apartment, walking to 125th Street to catch the train that would take me downtown. My days were long, starting early and not ending until 11 p.m., after finishing my tasks as an intern. It was a lot to manage, and eventually, I had to make the difficult decision to let the internship go, despite the connections I was making and the powerful people I was meeting in the fashion world.

Kenneth Cole, however, continued to be a solid foundation for me. My manager, someone I admired deeply, was a light in my workplace. She reminded me of my dad in some ways with her humor and leadership, and I looked up to her. She created a fair and supportive environment, something I hadn't experienced before in my working life. When she left Kenneth Cole, the morale of the team dropped, and I learned a valuable lesson about the power of leadership and how one person could shift the atmosphere of an entire space.

Then, one day, out of the blue, I got a call from her. She had been watching me closely during her time at Kenneth Cole, something I hadn't realized. She had taken a high-level position at Louis Vuitton and was now in a position to hire people she believed in. She told me that I fit the criteria for a role she was looking to fill. I was stunned. Louis Vuitton was a brand that represented the height of luxury, and she was offering me the chance to interview for a position there.

I remember sitting in a restaurant on 125th Street when she called, and after putting her on mute, I cried. Louis Vuitton is part of the LVMH group, a conglomerate that owns some of the most prestigious brands in the world. I thought about all the reasons I might not be deserving of this opportunity—my lack of polished clothing for an interview, my background, my self-doubt. But she reassured me that it was my personality and work ethic they were looking for, and everything else would work itself out.

The interview process was long and grueling. I spoke with representatives from the domestic team and even some from Paris. It was unlike anything I had ever experienced before, but I gave it my all, knowing that this could be life-changing. After months of interviewing, I received the call that I had been chosen. My manager-turned-mentor took me out to celebrate, and I was overwhelmed with gratitude. She had become one of my best friends and someone who had truly changed the course of my life.

On September 3, 2010, I started as the Client Relations Manager at Louis Vuitton. My first day felt like stepping into a movie. I was surrounded by luxury on a scale I had never known—shoes, trunks, travel bags, jewelry—all iconic pieces of a world I was now part of. The store I was working at had an inventory worth $80 million. It was hard to comprehend numbers like that, but I knew I had arrived in a new space, one that required me to rise to the occasion.

They provided tailored suits, polished shoes—everything I needed to step into this new role with confidence. But I knew that my presence there wasn't just by chance. My path had been guided by God, divinely driven by a purpose bigger than myself. I made a promise to immerse myself fully into this world, to learn from the people I would meet, and to take in all the experiences that were now unfolding before me. Every day brought in clients from all over the world, each one with a unique story, a new culture, something I could learn from. I knew this was just the beginning of something greater.

But amidst this newfound world of luxury and success, I found myself yearning to race back home to Baltimore. Life was balanced, and I was making money like never before—enough to not only support myself but to finally visit my family without worrying about the costs. 2010 was the first year I visited since departing. I'd have to say, it felt extremely different. It was the first time I was returning to Baltimore not out of necessity or struggle, but because I wanted to, because I was doing exactly what I had set out to do. Yet, this longing to go back when things were great puzzled me. Perhaps it was the need to share this version of myself with my family, to show them the good times, to let them see the growth and success firsthand. I wanted them to know that despite the distance and all the struggles, I was climbing up the corporate ladder, thriving in a city that often swallows people whole.

What they didn't see, what I never made a point to show, was the cost of those visits—the flights, ubers, rental cars, and hotels that added up to more than they could imagine. But none of that mattered when I saw them. All I knew was that I was in a better place, both financially and mentally, after working through so much trauma in therapy. I remember even inviting some family members to visit me in Harlem. I had an apartment ready to accommodate them, a space that symbolized the life I was building. But no one ever took me up on the offer. Despite the disappointment, I never allowed it to overshadow the pride I felt for being able to make that offer in the first place. For the first time, I was living in one of the greatest cities in the United States, and I wanted to share every part of it with those who had been there from the beginning, even if they couldn't or wouldn't see it. This longing to connect, to show them what I had achieved, was a part of the healing process—a way of reconciling where I had come from with where I was going.

The Transition Unveiled & The Blessing Embraced

The transition from Harlem's familiar streets to the luxury world of Louis Vuitton was not just about stepping into a new role—it was about finding my place in a world I never thought I could belong to. The blessing behind this transition was the understanding that sometimes we need others to see the greatness in us before we see it in ourselves. Through hard work, humility, and divine alignment, I embraced the fact that I was deserving of this new chapter, knowing that every step was leading me toward something greater.

Journal Entry

2011

I was 25, living in the city that promised dreams. New York, with its endless culture and diversity, had become my playground. The clubs at night, the people, the contacts—I was absorbing it all. Yet, I was always mindful of my manager and mentor's words from Kenneth Cole & Louis Vuitton: *"Reputation Is Key."* She had always been my guiding light through the maze of ambition and caution. At the start of the year, Sam called me and shared some life-changing news: she was pregnant. She had returned to Baltimore, a city she didn't truly want to be in, but circumstances had led her back. She wanted me to visit her during this significant time in her life. She loved having me by her side, or at least sharing in the joy of her journey. So, I took the Amtrak train home, a beautiful 4 hour ride, to spend time with her.

While I was there, we experienced the best time together, walking along Baltimore's Inner Harbor and eating at our favorite restaurant. Naturally, we indulged in as much seafood as possible being that we were in Baltimore— celebrating. It was a wonderful opportunity to not only support Sam but also to catch up and laugh about all our funniest moments from when we lived together in New York City.

We shared so many hysterical memories, and it felt like such a special time to reconnect.

While on this visit, I was emailed by my new job at Louis Vuitton requesting my presence in Paris for a three-month training program. It was an opportunity I couldn't afford to miss, a chance to immerse myself in a city that had already captured my imagination during my college years. Paris. The city of lights, the city of beauty and fashion— a place where one could dream and live in those dreams. While it was hard, I had to say goodbye to Sam. The next day, I packed my bags and left for New York, feeling both the excitement of a new adventure and the heaviness of the temporary goodbye.

As the Amtrak train sped toward New York, I watched the blurred landscape rush by, each mile pulling me closer to yet another leap into the unknown. My heart felt a strange mix of excitement and trepidation, the same way it always does before a big transition. The idea of living in Paris for three months—training, exploring, and rediscovering a place I hadn't seen since college—felt like the next great chapter in my life. But as exhilarating as it was, I couldn't ignore the twinge of uncertainty quietly sitting alongside it. Would I fit into a city so effortlessly stylish and steeped in culture? Did I even own clothes worthy of a Parisian sidewalk?

My mind raced as the train rocked gently beneath me, juggling practicalities like packing and itineraries alongside deeper reflections. I thought about how each transition, no matter how daunting, had shaped me in ways I couldn't fully appreciate at the time. This moment was no different—another layer of my story forming in real time. It wasn't sadness I felt, nor even fear, but rather an overwhelming awareness of the magnitude of change. Paris would undoubtedly leave its mark on me, as every new beginning has, and I'd carry its lessons long after my return. The clock was ticking—I had only 24 hours to prepare for a new life abroad—but even amidst the chaos, I found myself grateful for the opportunity to evolve yet again.

Paris was everything I hoped it would be and more. The city's rhythm was intoxicating. Mornings started with a flat white from a local café, and everyone—regardless of status—took a break between 12 and 2. It was perfectly normal to enjoy a glass of red wine during lunch, something I found liberating. The workdays stretched until 9 PM, but I hardly noticed the hours passing. My training was intense, demanding a meticulous eye for detail that I had never cultivated before. The Parisians insisted on it, and I learned to see the world in a new light, to notice the subtleties and nuances that gave life its texture.

My time couldn't end, without reconnecting with my old friend I had met during my first visit to Paris with the Morgan State University choir. He was delighted to find out I was in the city, and we spent time together whenever I could spare a moment. We explored the city and even traveled to Italy and London, broadening my horizons in ways I never thought possible. He was looking for something more serious, but I couldn't offer that. My focus had to remain on my work, on this incredible opportunity that had been laid before me. Our friendship thrived nonetheless, and he even introduced me to a world of sophistication that I had never known. He showed me the art of dining, from selecting the right napkin to the correct glass for each wine we were tasting throughout our evening together. These experiences were thrilling, yet tinged with the bittersweet awareness that I couldn't share these sentiments with my best friend, Sam.

During the time with him, I couldn't help but remember those days living with Sam in our small apartment in Spanish Harlem, New York. We'd spend hours sitting on that worn-out couch, daydreaming about someday visiting Paris together—indulging in the food, soaking in the culture, and wearing the latest fashions. Back then, Paris was more of a fantasy than a real destination, something we talked about to escape the noise and grind of the city around us. But like so many dreams, life had changed for both of us, pulling us in different directions. Still, those conversations stayed with me, etched in my memory, reminding me of a time when even the idea of Paris seemed like an impossible dream.

My time in Paris came to an end, and I had four days left before returning to New York. I was 25, and I wanted to live a little. I ventured into the gay neighborhood of Paris, seeking freedom and connection. There, in the middle of the loud techno music and surrounded by the beautiful Parisian men, I met an older gentleman—an American on vacation. He was an attorney, well-traveled, and with a longing for companionship that mirrored my own. We spent the next four days together, falling into a whirlwind romance that neither of us had anticipated. When it came time for me to leave, he surprised me with an offer: to fly back to New York with him on his private plane. He owned a home there, surprisedly only ten blocks from where I lived. I was stunned, caught between the thrill of the moment and the reality of what this meant.

Upon our return to New York, he invited me to his penthouse. I remember the elevator ride vividly, the press of the "PH" button, the realization of the life he led. It was a life so far removed from anything I had ever known, and yet, for a fleeting moment, I was a part of it. We shared a lovely dinner, listening to jazz—my favorite—and for the first time in months, I felt like I belonged. Yet, despite the allure, questions loomed in my mind. *Why me? What did he see in me that made him open his world to a young man like myself?*

As summer unfolded, I attended my first Gay Pride in New York. It was exhilarating, a celebration of identity and freedom unlike anything I had ever experienced. The attorney invited me to his annual Pride rooftop party, a glamorous affair that threw me into a world of opulence and excess. It was there, amidst the fancy cars, the security, the flashing lights, that I felt the full weight of my place in this world. For the first real time, I was aware of my race, of being the only gay Black man in the room. In Paris and Italy, interracial relationships were commonplace, but here, in the United States, it was different. It was a thing, a silent question that hung in the air. Although everyone seemed to know who I was, and while I enjoyed the attention, it also made me acutely aware of the delicate balance I was navigating.

I wasn't certain why it was this way. By this point in my life, I had traveled extensively and witnessed how, in many other countries, relationships between older men and younger men seemed to be accepted—or at least not met with the same scrutiny. But as I stood at the party, enjoying myself, I couldn't help but notice the looks from others around my age. Their expressions, filled with a mix of disgust and judgment, lingered in the air, making me question everything in that moment. Was it me? Was it my outfit? Or was it the age difference between me and the man I had come to see? The weight of those stares pressed on me, and I found myself trying to piece it all together, searching for answers. Why was judgment so readily handed out, even in spaces that were meant to be safe? Why did it feel like I was being asked to justify simply being there?

As the night wore on, the party took a turn. I noticed the drugs making their rounds, and suddenly, I was transported back to a place I had fought hard to leave behind. The allure of his world was intoxicating, but I knew the price. I had worked too hard to get to where I was. I couldn't go back. I completely distanced myself, knowing that while this man offered me a life of luxury, it was a life that could easily consume me.

During this whirlwind summer, my mother got married. It was July 1, 2011, a date that marked a turning point in our fractured relationship. We hadn't spoken since 2007 when I left for college against her wishes. Those four years of silence had been heavy, a lingering shadow over my life.

But now, I was being offered a chance to reconnect. The attorney allowed me to use his plane to fly to Baltimore for the wedding. It was a surreal experience, arriving in such style to witness my mother embark on a new chapter of her own. For the first time in years, I felt a glimmer of hope for our relationship.

To witness the magic in my mother's eyes—not for the first time, but in a way that felt profound and enduring—was a gift I will always treasure. I was overwhelmed with happiness for her as she found love with a wonderful Black man who treated her like the queen she had always deserved to be. He was the polar opposite of what I had known her to endure in the past—relationships marked by verbal and physical abuse that chipped away at her spirit. But this man, this genuine, hard-working African-American man, restored a light in her that had always been there but hadn't always been nurtured. I could not have been more overjoyed to see her embrace this new chapter, this new stage of life that pointed in a direction filled with respect, love, and a quiet strength she so richly deserved.

Witnessing all this, felt like a life I barely understood, but one I felt I deserved after everything I had been through. Yet, as glamorous as it all was, I felt the emptiness creeping in. When Thanksgiving and Christmas came that year, I found myself alone. The attorney was in San Francisco, and I was left in New York, surrounded by the vibrant city lights but isolated from the warmth of family. In the quiet moments of those holidays, I realized something profound: despite all the luxury and excitement, I longed for something deeper, something more real. I wanted to share these moments with someone who truly knew me, not just the persona I had crafted in these glamorous settings. I had seen so much, experienced so many facets of life, but I was still searching for that elusive connection, that place where I could truly be myself without pretense or expectation.

2011 was a year of lessons, of testing my boundaries, and of discovering what truly mattered to me. It was a year that taught me that not all that glitters is gold, and sometimes, the most valuable experiences are those that challenge us to look within and confront the truths we've been avoiding. It was in the City of Lights and the Big Apple that I began to see the world—and myself—with a clarity I had never known before.

The Transition Unveiled & The Blessing Embraced

2011 was a year of immense growth and transformation for me. While I experienced incredible highs—living in Paris, working in luxury fashion, and being part of a world that seemed so far from my past—I also faced the reality of what was missing in my life. The transition was not just about stepping into a new world but about learning how to balance it with the deep emotional scars I still carried. The blessing was in the realization that while I had been running from my past, I was also running toward a future where I could define myself on my own terms, even if that journey required me to face the emptiness I sometimes felt inside.

Journal Entry

2012

The year began with an air of heaviness. Thanksgiving and Christmas of 2011 had left me feeling unsettled, the weight of loneliness in a big city pressing down on me. I was surrounded by new experiences, new people, and new cultures, and had a job that many would envy. Yet, the saying, *"If you don't have anyone to share it with, then why are you doing it?"* began to resonate with me more deeply than ever before. Journeying home for mother's wedding a year prior, stirred up old traumas I thought I had tucked away. It baffled me how people could carry on with life, ignoring the unhealed wounds of the past. Attending her wedding was surreal. It felt as if nothing had ever happened, like the unresolved pain was a figment of my imagination. I knew, I had done the work on myself, but this seemed to be my family's way—burying issues beneath a facade of normalcy, carrying on as if everything was fine.

I carried the burden of this emotional turmoil into 2012. My mind was restless, laden with the silent expectations of unspoken family history. But amidst this heaviness, a small glimmer of hope appeared. A dear friend from my past at the Arena Players Youth Theater and Baltimore School for the Arts shared the news that he was moving from Astoria to Harlem, just nine blocks away from me. In a city where finding genuine connection felt like searching for a needle in a haystack, knowing he would be close brought me comfort. He became my emergency contact, the one I could rely on if things went south. More than that, he understood where I came from—my history, my struggles, and my identity. As a homosexual himself, he shared my experiences and fears, and it was freeing to have someone who truly saw me. He was thriving in his acting career, gracing Broadway and stages across New York, and he welcomed me into his world. He was like family to me, even though we weren't related by blood. In him, I found a sense of belonging.

While he thrived in his field, my path was different. I was not born with the luxury of chasing my dreams without the safety net of a steady job. My upbringing had taught me the necessity of stability. So, I held onto my 9-to-5, securing benefits, a 401(k), dental and vision insurance, and a consistent paycheck. My family, with their limited life experiences, could not understand the complexities of the life I was building. Conversations with them felt foreign, like trying to translate my world into a language they did not speak. I soon realized that their jealousy, though painful, was rooted in their own limitations. They had never ventured out of Baltimore, never dreamed beyond their immediate surroundings.

Work became increasingly demanding, and I found myself barely holding on during this time. I needed something to ground me, to offer me a sense of peace amidst the growing chaos. In my search for balance, I discovered Jivamukti Yoga School in Union Square. I had often shopped at the Whole Foods there and would notice people leaving the yoga school above, glowing with an inner light despite being drenched in sweat. I longed for that radiance, that sense of peace. I had dabbled in yoga before and knew its transformative power, so I decided to make Jivamukti my sanctuary, my church. The moment I stepped into that space, I was enveloped by the scent of eucalyptus, the warmth of the room, and the soothing music that called me inward. The people were kind, radiating a sense of community that I had longed for. Jivamukti became my daily ritual, a place where I could shed the layers of stress and tension that accumulated throughout my days. The practice reshaped me, not just mentally but physically as well. It was a renewal of my spirit. The discipline of yoga led me to embrace vegetarianism, a choice that aligned with the teachings of respecting the temple that is my body.

Before finding this practice, my diet was far from healthy. I was constantly on the go, often unable to afford the healthiest foods. Convenience took precedence, and I found myself consuming a lot of red meat—pork, beef—anything that would fill me up quickly. But I began to notice how those foods made me feel—heavy, sluggish, and disconnected from my body. As I delved deeper into understanding food and its impact, I started reading about how much of the food in the United States was pumped with hormones and preservatives, substances that were doing more harm than good to my body.

With my changed diet, I experienced a transformation in just one month. My entire body felt better. I had more energy, my skin cleared up, and the discoloration on my face vanished. My teeth and hair became healthier, reflecting the internal changes taking place. It became crystal clear to me that we are what we put into our bodies. The body is only reacting to what we feed it and how we treat it.

March 12, 2012, that year —amidst the whirlwind of work, I was called into the office and was informed of my promotion. It was a moment of triumph, recognition for my dedication and hard work. Yet, with this newfound promotion came even greater responsibility. The demands on my time and energy grew exponentially. However, I ensured that my weekends were still often filled with travel, sometimes to be with my family/friends, sometimes simply to find peace-of-mind elsewhere— outside the city. The attorney I was involved with encouraged this constant movement, and while I craved companionship, I also knew I needed to focus on my career. My mentor, a guiding light in my professional journey, called me one Friday night to share that she was leaving Louis Vuitton after four years. Her departure left, yet another void, another loss in a pattern of happiness followed by departure that had haunted me since childhood.

I started to notice, when loss or departure happens in my life, it triggers something within, reminding me of the importance of confronting childhood trauma head-on. Jivamukti was my anchor during these times, offering a space where I could process my pain. Still, a part of me missed my family, despite the unresolved tensions and traumas. I reached out to the attorney, asking if I could use his plane to visit Baltimore. He accompanied me, spending time in the city while I visited my family. My grandmother's house (my mother's mother), nestled in the countryside of Baltimore, was beautiful and serene, a stark contrast to the loud disagreements and arguing that often erupted within its walls. The familiar arguments and unresolved issues resurfaced, making me question why I kept returning in search of love only to be met with pain.

Eventually, I grew tired of the constant emotional upheaval. The attorney and I began spending weekends in Japan, exploring a culture that fascinated both of us. It was an escape from the emotional turmoil of home and the relentless pace of my career. However, the calls from my family persisted, filled with requests for help or favors, but rarely checking on my well-being. They seemed oblivious to the fact that I was in the prime of my career, struggling to balance the demands of my professional and personal life.

In the end, I made a vow to myself. I was willing to embrace solitude if it meant building a life of my own design. The journey was mine to navigate, and I could not allow myself to be anchored by the limitations of others.

The Transition Unveiled & The Blessing Embraced

In 2012, I grappled with the complex reality of family, solitude, and the pursuit of inner peace. The transition this year unveiled was the courage to seek sanctuary within myself rather than in the tumultuous and often unpredictable dynamics of my family and surroundings. Through the solace of Jivamukti Yoga School, the unexpected joy of reconnecting with chosen family, and the trials of balancing personal growth with career ambitions, I embraced the blessing of self-awareness and the journey toward inner harmony.

Journal Entry

2013

2013 was a chapter of realization for me because at 27, despite many considering that age to be young, I felt like I had lived the experiences of someone much older. Life had forced me to grow up quickly, and my reality at 27 felt more like 40. This year, I found myself on the brink of another promotion, but it was different this time. My mentor, the one who had always ensured I was properly compensated and protected, was no longer there to advocate for me. I was being promoted to a larger role with more responsibilities and more employees to oversee, but something about it just didn't sit right. I had multiple meetings with my direct report as well as various executives within the company, and although I took the promotion, it was with a heavier heart this time. I couldn't shake the feeling that I wasn't being valued or seen for what I was truly worth, and it left a bitter taste in my mouth. Still, I took the opportunity because I needed the money, but my excitement was tempered with frustration.

Work became more demanding and all-consuming, leaving me with no personal life. I knew things were bad when I couldn't even attend my spiritual and emotional outlet— Jivamukti Yoga School as frequently as I had been. My relationship with the attorney, which had been such a source of comfort, began to crumble. We started arguing more frequently, not because we didn't care about each other, but because our lives were no longer aligning. He was his own boss, with endless free time, while I had to report to mine. Our final trip was to Dubai as he needed to report there for work— it was the saddest trip. As we boarded his private jet that had once been a symbol of luxury and freedom, I knew it would be the last time. The whole trip felt heavy, as if the weight of the impending end overshadowed everything. I loved Dubai, and I loved that he took me on that trip with him, but I also knew it may not have been the perfect place for us considering our current state. The culture there didn't allow for us to be openly gay, and I felt constrained, unable to express myself fully. It was strange that he chose to take me with him to Dubai, a place that had so many limitations. The limitations of what we could do and say in such a strict environment only added to the sadness of the trip.

I returned to New York knowing the relationship was over and that I was back to square one in my search for connection.

Not long after that year, the company selected me to be part of the US Open tennis tournament that was being held in New York City that year. It was a major event, and I jumped at the opportunity to be on this committee, hoping it would help me refocus on work and not on the breakup. It was at the tournament, that I met a tennis writer who worked for *The Times* (based in London). He was captivating—so much so that during our conversation, his boss even asked if he was paying attention to the tennis match for his article. We exchanged numbers, and he invited me to have a drink at his hotel after the event. I was hesitant at first, still nursing the pain from my breakup with the attorney, but something about him was different. He stayed in New York longer than he had planned just to spend more time with me, and we explored the city together—attending the opera, the ballet, and discovering piano bars I never knew existed in New York City.

Our bond deepened, and before long, we were flying back and forth between New York and London. It felt like a whirlwind, but it also made me wonder why I always seemed to attract powerful, older, white men. Was it my maturity? Was it that I was wise beyond my years? Or was I still trying to heal my *"daddy issues"* from years of neglect and unresolved trauma? Regardless, I never questioned their kindness. After everything I had been through, I just wanted to be treated well.

During one of our trips, I confided in him about the mistreatment I had ensured during the negotiation process of my recent promotion, and started to feel undervalued at Louis Vuitton. In his wise words, he encouraged me to apply for a new position that felt far out of my reach—one I would have never considered on my own. His belief in me was stronger than my self-doubt, and I finally mustered the courage to take his advice. Six months later, I sent in my application, waited for the third interview to be completed, then I put in my two weeks' notice at Louis Vuitton as I knew I had gotten the new job.

While December 2013 marked a pivotal turning point in my life. I still remember the mix of emotions I felt as I hit "send" on my resignation email, addressing it to the very person who had failed to recognize my worth and continuously undervalued me in my role. It wasn't just about this one individual—it was about the realization that often, in major corporations, you're seen as a number rather than a human being. Working for Louis Vuitton had been an incredible experience in many ways, but it also revealed the challenges of navigating a corporate structure that often feels impersonal and mechanical, driven by countless departments and layers of bureaucracy. There was no bitterness toward the brand itself—it's a massive machine, after all—but it was clear to me that this machine was no longer a space where I could thrive. In that moment, I knew I had to walk away from Louis Vuitton for good, trusting that this decision would lead me to something more aligned with who I was and who I was becoming.

The Transition Unveiled & The Blessing Embraced

As 2013 came to a close, I realized that sometimes, the end of one chapter is simply a necessary step toward a more fulfilling future. Despite the disappointments, the exhaustion, and the broken relationships, I found the courage to walk away from what no longer served me. I embraced the transition and trusted that my journey would continue to lead me toward growth, even when the path felt uncertain. The blessing of this year was not just the new job—it was learning to value myself enough to demand more from life.

Journal Entry

2014

As 2014 dawned, I found myself standing at a crossroads. My time at Louis Vuitton had come to an end, a chapter closing that left me with a whirlwind of emotions. The going-away party they threw for me was lovely, filled with familiar faces that wore expressions of sadness. We had built something more than just a team; we had become a family. There was an unspoken bond, a camaraderie that made the farewell bittersweet. They wanted me to stay, even the upper management approached me during the celebration, asking if I would reconsider. But I knew my worth. At 27, I was at a juncture where I needed to stand up for myself, to not settle for less than what I deserved.

January 5th marked my last day, and though it was difficult to walk away, I had made a commitment to myself. I had already signed on with a startup company set to begin on January 15th. The allure of a fresh opportunity and the promise of a broader role with more responsibilities beckoned me. This new venture in contemporary fashion was a stark departure from the world of luxury I had grown accustomed to. It seemed like the perfect next step to diversify my portfolio, but as life often teaches, things are not always as they seem.

When I finally stepped into this new role, it became painfully clear that what was presented to me on paper was not the reality I was stepping into. This was a profound lesson in business and life—one that taught me the importance of being crystal clear about expectations, contracts, and the value of having legal counsel to scrutinize the fine print. I found myself in an environment that clashed with everything I had known. The workplace culture was different, almost hostile at times. My background in luxury fashion seemed to intimidate my colleagues, leading to an undercurrent of jealousy and unnecessary cattiness. The environment became increasingly uncomfortable, filled with micromanagement and a sense of distrust that was foreign to me.

By April, just four months in, the strain of it all had begun to weigh heavily on me. I was trying to fit into a "world" that wasn't ready to accept me, not in the way I was or the way I operated. I vividly remember that year I went to have lunch with a friend in the heart of beautiful Soho, New York where the job was located. We chose to sit outside because, if you know anything about New York summers, you know how magical they are—especially in Soho. The cobblestone streets were alive with people bouncing around in the latest fashions, their energy as vibrant as the art galleries, boutique stores, coffee shops, and restaurants that surrounded us. Soho felt like the epitome of beauty and culture, a living canvas of style and inspiration.

As we lingered over our delicious lunch, soaking in the rhythm of the city, my friend made an observation that struck a chord. He pointed out how, for years, I had been grinding nonstop, always chasing, always striving, rarely allowing myself to let loose or embrace the freedom of simply being. His words lingered with me, stirring a quiet reflection. In that moment, I realized how much I had been denying myself the joy of truly living, of pausing to appreciate the life I was building in a city as alive as I wanted to feel. Here I was, in one of the biggest cities in the United States, yet I hadn't fully embraced the opportunities for connection and growth outside of work.

Taking my friend's advice, I decided to step outside my comfort zone. I joined dating apps, including Grindr. Despite its reputation, I approached it with an open mind, hoping to meet someone genuine— and I did. The connection was different, unfamiliar in a way that felt strangely good. Up to this point, my romantic relationships had been with older, powerful white men. This new connection, however, was vibrant and full of a youthful energy that I hadn't experienced before. He was younger, less structured, and obsessed with Black culture—a culture I had often felt somewhat disconnected from, given my experiences.

Our relationship was a juxtaposition of worlds. While he was fascinated by the idea of an African-American man indulging in what he perceived as typical cultural norms, I had long moved away from those expectations. My life had been one of constant change, guided by the pursuit of growth and new experiences that often took me beyond the boundaries of my upbringing. The conversations we had were both enlightening and challenging. They forced me to confront the nuances of my identity, the reasons behind my choices, and the societal expectations I had spent my life either embracing or rebelling against.

As the months passed, I navigated both the complexities of this new friendship and the turmoil at work. The tension at the startup reached a breaking point, and by September, I was called into the headquarters in Midtown. It was clear that things weren't working out. We mutually agreed that it was best for me to bow out gracefully. For the first time in my life, I was leaving a job without another one lined up. The fear of the unknown was paralyzing, yet a part of me felt an odd sense of liberation.

In a moment of vulnerability, I confided in the man I had been dating. Even though it felt too soon to share such personal information, I've always believed that being open and transparent is the key to building any meaningful relationship. We were still in the early stages of getting to know one another, but I felt it was important to share this news with him—if things were to deepen, he needed to be in the know. To my surprise, my honesty opened a door for him to do the same. He admitted that he, too, was struggling—facing challenges at work that were weighing heavily on him. In that moment, I couldn't help but feel a sense of *awe*. What were the odds that I would find myself sharing such a parallel experience with someone I was just beginning to care for? For a brief moment, I thought, *Wow, maybe this is meant to be.*

As we continued to talk and learn more about one another, it became clear that our lives had even more in common than we initially realized. We found ourselves bonding over the shared realities of living in New York: the relentless hustle and bustle, the chaos of crowded trains, the sweltering heat of summer, and the bone-chilling cold of snowy winters. Those conversations slowly began to reveal something deeper—we were both sensing the need for a change—a transition. Inevitably, the topic shifted toward the West Coast, a place we both spoke about with a sense of longing and curiosity. It was as if the universe was nudging us in the same direction, gently suggesting that a new chapter was waiting for both of us, perhaps together, or perhaps as part of our individual journeys.

It was then that I reached out to my mentor, the same one who had left Louis Vuitton before I resigned. When I told her about my predicament, she responded with an enthusiasm I hadn't expected. She revealed that she had been looking for someone to fill a position in the Los Angeles branch of a luxury brand, and hadn't approached me before out of respect for my commitment to the startup she thought I was still working at. It felt as though the universe had conspired in my favor, guiding me toward a path that I couldn't have foreseen.

In that moment, I remembered, my steps are divinely guided. Even though I didn't always understand the *"why"* behind each transition, I had learned to trust the process. This new opportunity was more than a job offer; it was a sign that I was on the right path, even if that path was still shrouded in uncertainty.

The whirlwind of events led to a rapid escalation in my now— *new relationship*. Over the next few months, we traveled together, met each other's families, and began making plans for a future that seemed both thrilling and precarious. His world was different from mine—luxurious, guarded, and somewhat disconnected from the reality I knew. Meeting his family brought a new layer of complexity. Their wealth and status cast a shadow of expectation, and for the first time, I questioned my integrity and whether I was willing to compromise my values for the promise of a life that felt both alluring and alien.

By December 2014, I had made up my mind. I purchased my first car and began making plans for the move to Los Angeles. We decided to ship our cars to California, following the advice of his parents, who were deeply involved in every aspect of our transition. The entire experience was surreal, pushing me to question the nature of love, sacrifice, and the pursuit of a life that felt right for me.

On December 31st, at 6:14 PM, we boarded a flight to Los Angeles, California. We planned it meticulously to arrive just before the stroke of midnight, toasting to a new year and a new chapter in the air. As the plane ascended, so did my hopes for what awaited on the West Coast. We touched down on January 1, 2015, ready to embrace the adventure that lay ahead.

The Transition Unveiled & The Blessing Embraced

This chapter was a testament to the unpredictable nature of life's transitions. What began as the end of one career path transformed into an unforeseen journey of self-discovery and growth. The challenges and discomfort I faced in this period revealed not just the harsh realities of navigating the professional world but also the intricate dynamics of relationships and personal values. The blessing behind this transition was the clarity it provided—showing me the importance of trusting in the process, even when the path ahead seems unclear. In stepping into the unknown, I was being prepared for a life that was richer, more diverse, and deeply aligned with the person I was becoming.

Journal Entry

2015

California greeted us with open arms and uncertainty. It was January 1, 2015, and as we stepped out of the uber, the sight of our cars waiting outside my closest friend's home filled me with a sense of accomplishment. We had made it. My friend had been my confidante since our days at Berklee, a bridesmaid at her wedding, and now, she welcomed us into her California life with trust and warmth. She wasn't home that day, away for the holidays, yet she had prepared our room with a photo of us and two glasses of wine. It was a simple gesture that spoke volumes about the depth of our friendship and the trust she placed in us.

I couldn't quite believe the path I was on, especially with a man I had met just ten months prior. Here I was, introducing him to those closest to my heart, weaving him into the fabric of my life. On January 3rd, after days of searching for apartments and getting our bearings, we found ourselves deep in conversation. We had packed our lives into our cars, shipped from the East Coast, as a cost-effective way to transport everything we owned. We had two months to find a place before my new job at Chloé started on March 1. It was crucial to find a location that minimized my commute since I had heard the horror stories about California traffic.

When the topic shifted to budget, a conversation about money– a natural stress point in any relationship– he said something that sent chills down my spine: *"I need to talk to my parents."* At that moment, standing in my friend's living room in Van Nuys, I felt a sinking realization. Was I with someone who still needed to consult his parents for every financial decision? I had already moved my life across the country, signed a contract with Chloé, and set everything in motion. There was no turning back.

I tried not to judge him for consulting his family; after all, this was the world he was used to. But the reality was stark: I was in a relationship not just with him, but, with his parents as well. I found us an apartment in Beverly Hills, a choice that raised eyebrows for its expense, but I knew proximity to work was non-negotiable. With my determination, we moved in eight days after arriving. It felt like I was doing all the heavy lifting on my own. He came from money, but without his parents' direct support, he had nothing of his own. They funded his life, requiring him to itemize every expense. It was a dance that left me frustrated, but what could I do? We were here now.

The months of January and February were a whirlwind of fun. We tired to explore everything California had to offer – from the valleys of Van Nuys and Toluca Lake to the sun-soaked beaches of Malibu, Santa Monica, and Venice Beach. We drove to Palm Springs and Las Vegas, savoring the beauty and excitement of our new surroundings. For a brief moment, the thrill of adventure masked the tension beneath the surface.

When March 1st arrived, I began my new role at Chloé on Melrose Place in West Hollywood, California. It was a return to luxury, a familiar and comforting world under the umbrella of Richemont. To those who understand luxury, Richemont and LVMH stand as titans of the industry, coveted affiliations for anyone in the field. My mentor had always known what was best for me, and now, I felt at home again. The team welcomed me warmly, and the California lifestyle, free from the burden of snow and rain, was a breath of fresh air. My role allowed me to meet a plethora of famous and powerful individuals, expanding my network and offering me a glimpse into the world of Hollywood.

Yet, amidst this professional high, I grappled with the reality of my relationship. He was a trust-fund baby, shielded by the cushion of his parents' wealth. By this time, we were settled in our new Beverly Hills apartment and it was time to furnish it. When I suggested we start to buy some furniture, his response was always the same: *"I don't have any money."* It was a pattern. Every decision, every purchase, every plan for our future required a consultation with his parents. I soon discovered, he didn't even know how to write a check or understand credit. It dawned on me that I was not just older than him in years, but also in life experience.

By this time, I had poured myself into my work, climbing the corporate ladder, growing my clientele, and sharing my story of transition from New York to California with everyone I was meeting. During my exchange of telling my story of transition, many advised me to walk away from this relationship, but I couldn't. I had separation issues. Walking away felt like another failure, another person walking out of my life— another thing I couldn't keep.

As the year progressed, the holidays approached– our first together. His parents had funded much of his life, and I was determined to show them what we had built. I took pride in hosting them, drawing on my training from a course I had taken in Paris on *"The Art of Hosting."* Our one-bedroom apartment in Beverly Hills couldn't accommodate them, so they stayed nearby at the Sofitel Hotel. I prepared everything meticulously, hoping to impress them and make them comfortable. The visit was a display, a showcase of our life, and they seemed impressed with what we had managed to create.

But beneath this polished exterior lay a troubling dynamic. His father was secretly funneling money to him, unbeknownst to his stepmother. I was complicit in this secrecy, bound to keep the family's affairs private. I was living in a relationship with layers of complexity, where the boundaries between love, support, and control were blurred. I couldn't fault anyone but myself. I had chosen this path, this person. I had committed to a life where every decision involved not just him but his parents as well.

As the clock struck midnight on New Year's Eve, ushering in January 2016, I couldn't shake the feeling of being in over my head. This was not the life I had envisioned when I moved to California.

The Transition Unveiled & The Blessing Embraced

2015 was a year of bold moves and unforeseen realities. The transition to California unveiled the complexities of love, independence, and the price of compromise. It revealed the intricate dance between pursuing personal dreams and navigating a relationship that wasn't just between two people but was interwoven with the influence of others. The blessing in this transition lay in the clarity it brought—a deeper understanding of what I was willing to accept and the strength I possessed to carve out a life on my own terms, even amidst uncertainty. This chapter was a testament to resilience, learning to navigate a world that wasn't always aligned with my vision but still held lessons that would guide me forward.

Journal Entry

2016

In 2016, his parents had finally left. It was just the two of us, and it was then that I began to feel like I was no longer in a relationship with a partner but with a son. I know how that might sound, but it was not literal. Our dynamic had shifted into one where I was the sole provider—organizing all the bills, ensuring there was food on the table, helping him with his résumé, trying to connect him with job opportunities— and so much more. It was as though every responsibility rested on me. I had never been in a relationship like this before, one that left me feeling more like a guardian than a partner.

The more this pattern settled in, the more my affection for him faded. All the dreams we had shared, all the conversations about our future back in New York City before our move to California, now seemed empty. The disconnect grew to the point where our arguments became physical. That was a line I never thought we'd cross. As an African-American gay man, I was acutely aware of how this would be perceived by others, especially his parents and of course if authorizes were ever called. In their eyes, any fault would be mine. The fear of this judgment weighed on me, pushing me further into isolation. I began spending more and more time outside of our apartment because I could no longer handle the constant conflicts. In his eyes, it was arguing, but to me, it felt like I was fighting for the survival of a household, for the remnants of what we had.

He never understood the demands of my work. I was often exhausted from my job, coming home tired yet still trying to find the energy to make him happy. He had always had his parents as a safety net, but I had no such luxury. I was trying to build a life from the ground up, far from the familiarity and life I had known on the East Coast.

With all this tension on my plate, I felt the familiar urge to numb the situation, to fall back into old habits, but I resisted. Instead, I turned to what I knew could ground me: yoga. I joined Hot 8 Yoga in Beverly Hills, a place much like Jivamukti Yoga School had been for me in New York. Yoga became my refuge once more, a place where I could find balance and reconnect with myself. It was my church, and in the studio, I sought peace. I stayed away from the apartment as much as possible, only returning when it was time to sleep. I found myself immersed in the beauty of California, a world where the sky felt like the limit.

In an effort to find some joy, I attended a performance at the Blue Note in Hollywood. My theater teacher, who had become my godfather, was managing a brilliant jazz singer, and he invited me to the show. Watching her perform sparked something within me, a reminder of the dreams and passions that had once fueled me. For a moment, I was transported back to a time when life felt full of possibilities. Yet, no one in the Blue Note had any idea about the turmoil I was enduring in my life, the battles I was fighting behind closed doors.

After the concert, on April 15, 2016, I returned to an almost empty apartment. He had left. I collapsed onto the floor, overwhelmed by the weight of abandonment. I wept until there were no more tears, my sobs echoing in the emptiness of our shared space. How could he just walk out on everything we had built together? We had made plans, bought cars together, moved across the country. I felt betrayed and lost, as if the ground beneath me had crumbled. In the weeks that followed, I struggled to piece myself back together. I turned heavily to journaling, a practice that had been a lifeline for me since my time at Jivamukti Yoga School in New York. Writing became my outlet, a place where I could confront my emotions. But I still was numb. I didn't want to be in any kind of intimate relationship anytime soon— or ever again. His departure meant I was left to face the daunting reality of handling everything on my own. What's interesting is that, his father was helping him, which in turn helped the household, it was only a fraction of what was needed. My family back home couldn't offer support; they were too busy asking for it from me. They needed me to be the anchor, the one to fly home, the one to provide. They never once paused to consider what I was going through in my daily life.

So, as I had done so many times before, I buried myself in work and yoga. I kept my head down, knowing that running from problems was not the answer. I turned to God, asking what lesson I was meant to learn from this, getting silent in the moments that felt the hardest to bear. The teachings of my childhood church started to resurface in my mind, reminding me to seek strength from a higher power when my own had run dry.

I began working more hours and took on extra activities to fill the void. I reached out to people I had met through my job, including celebrities who introduced me to a world of luxury lunches and dinners. They took me to places like *Château Marmont on Sunset Boulevard* and *Soho House in West Hollywood*, spots that became my new stomping grounds. I kept myself busy, trying to drown out the hurt.

At one point, I even called the attorney I had met in Paris, thinking maybe now that I was in California (closer to San Francisco where his other home was located), we could pickup where we left off as friends. But he had moved on, found someone else, and was living his life. So, I kept going through my past roster also contacting the tennis writer who was back in London, but during that call, he revealed that he needed to call me back because he was amongst his wife and two daughters whom I never knew existed. He had a secret life back in London, adding another layer of stress to my already burdened shoulders.

Taking this all in, I knew it was time to get to know myself in way I hadn't done before. So, I started traveling—alone. Returning to places that had once brought me joy, seeking solace in the memories of a time when I felt whole. New York and Boston were my escapes. It was in Boston, during a conversation with a mentor, that I was encouraged to seek another therapist. This mentor was a dear teacher and friend whom I had met at Berklee College of Music. A powerful singer, she was highly revered at Berklee, with even a stairwell named after her in honor of her impact on the school. We had grown very close over the years, and she became one of my strongest supporters. I remember her telling me, *"Maybe it's time to switch therapists. You've had your therapist for quite some time, and it's good to change things up. You need a non-biased opinion, someone to talk to."* Her words resonated with me, making me realize that perhaps a fresh perspective was what I needed to navigate the complexities of these new emotions.

And so, I did just that— got a new therapist. As the year came to a close that year, Christmas 2016 felt different. I had asked my new therapist if we could have a session on December 25th (in an effect to not be alone that year). The holiday was hard for me. I was alone. I took out the Christmas tree we had bought together, but everything felt hollow. Life was supposed to be shared, yet here I was, trying to find a new path.

In the months that followed, I began to shift my perspective on life. I had turned 30 that year, on August 9th. I told myself that what ended on April 15th had to be a turning point for the good. I was working so hard to find meaning in shared moments, to approach new relationships in the most healthiest ways, but during that time, I still felt I needed more time to be with myself. I vowed not to let bitterness take root in my heart. God had been too good to me for me to become bitter by anything life had presented. I chose to use this time to heal, to grow, and to redefine what I wanted from life moving forward.

But, during this time, I couldn't stop thinking about my past relationships, one thought in particular kept resurfacing: were my experiences with older white men easier, not because of their person, but because of how I moved through those relationships? I couldn't help but wonder if the ease came from a space of internalized acceptance, or perhaps, from something much deeper. In New York City, I often felt a sense of discomfort being seen with them—walking beside these older men, aware of the stares and silent judgments from those around us. It wasn't uncommon to receive side-eye glances, whispers, or knowing looks that implied I was on the arm of a *'sugar daddy.'* Society's assumptions felt so loud in those moments, but the truth was much quieter and far more profound: these were genuine connections, matches that felt as though they were meant to be. Yet, no matter how deep that bond was, the weight of external judgment was always present.

I find myself now looking back and asking a question I hadn't fully considered before: was I letting the world's view of me shape my own? Was I more focused on what others thought than on what made me truly happy? These moments of reflection brought a flood of emotions, as I dissected each relationship through a different lens— wondering how much of my choices were influenced by societal expectations versus my own heart. It's a complicated truth, one that still lingers in my mind. In the end, perhaps the most important question isn't what others see, but whether I was truly content with who I was and how I loved.

The Transition Unveiled & The Blessing Embraced

This chapter marked a profound transition—a shift from dependency and the loss of a relationship that once held so much promise to a solitary journey of self-reliance and inner strength. In the departure of someone I had believed to be my partner, I was forced to confront the reality of standing alone. It was a painful awakening, one that left me questioning my own worth and the sacrifices I had made for a love that didn't last.

Yet, within this tumultuous period, there was a blessing. The pain of his departure pushed me to seek healing in places that had always been my sanctuary—yoga, writing, and the silent conversations with God that guided me toward understanding and growth. In losing what I thought was my future, I gained a deeper connection to myself. I learned that while life is meant to be shared, there is strength in learning to stand alone, to find joy and purpose within oneself before extending it to others. This chapter was not just about the end of a relationship; it was about the rebirth of my spirit, the awakening of a new perspective on love, self-worth, and the endless possibilities that lie in the path of transition.

Journal Entry

2017

2017 was a year of settling, adapting, and navigating a world that felt both familiar and foreign. By this point, I had begun to find my rhythm in Los Angeles. I knew where to go for what I needed and was getting used to the perpetual sunshine and warm weather, a stark contrast to the East Coast life I had left behind. There was no snow, no rain, just the endless cycle of 70, 80, 90-degree days. It was a lifestyle shift, one that I was learning to embrace. Being single, I was trying to navigate this new world on my own while ensuring I stayed on top of my job, which had been going smoothly for the past two years at this point. Work was stable, and nothing seemed out of place—until it was.

One day, as I walked into my job, a colleague pulled me aside. He was a manager at Oscar de la Renta, right next door to where I worked at Chloe'. He hesitated before asking, *"Did you and your partner break up?"* I was taken aback. By nature, I was a private person, especially after everything I had been through. Social media was beginning to change the world, branding and marketing oneself were becoming essential, but I wasn't ready to expose my personal life to that degree. I hadn't even told my friends about the breakup, but I felt compelled to be honest in that moment. *"Yes, we're no longer together,"* I confided, asking him to keep this between us.

He nodded solemnly and then shared why he had asked. *"I found your ex on Grindr,"* he said, referring to the app where we had first met back in New York. Shock washed over me. Here I was, still trying to process the end of our relationship, and he was already back on the app, searching for something—or someone—new. It became clear where he stood in his life, and it forced me to confront the reality of mine.

I lived five minutes from my workplace, and his new apartment was only four blocks away from our old place. The proximity of our professional lives complicated things further. I emailed him, called him, asking him to respect my request to stay off the app. My exact words were: *"Respectfully, what are you doing on this app— begging other men for sex? We are now moving into a direction of professionalism in our careers, and I can't bare you being on the app looking/begging for sex. Please, show me some respect as I continue to navigate my career in Los Angeles."* His response was swift and dismissive. He refused to listen, asserting that he could do whatever he wanted.

Two weeks later, I was at work, leading a meeting, when two sheriffs walked into the store. They halted the meeting, and everyone's face turned to me, their expressions a mixture of confusion and concern. The sheriff called out, *"I'm looking for Jordan Brown."* My heart sank as I acknowledged, *"That's me."* Sweat poured down my face as I excused myself from the meeting. The sheriff handed me a stack of papers—a temporary restraining order filed by my ex, accusing me of harassment through the emails I had sent pleading for him to stop his actions on the app.

This was a first for me, yet with everything you've read so far, you can imagine that I was prepared for just about anything by now. I had to dig into my savings to hire an attorney, a costly endeavor in a state like California. Nearly all my savings were depleted, and on top of that, I was shouldering all the household bills alone since he departed. It felt like the walls were closing in on me, and the person I once loved had placed me in this nightmare.

I returned to work that day, shattered and embarrassed. I had no choice but to explain the situation to my boss and colleagues, admitting that my personal life had intruded on my professional one in the most devastating way. After requesting the rest of the day off, I went home and allowed myself to cry. But I only gave myself that day. I knew I had to pull myself together by the next morning. *"Remember who you are,"* I told myself. *"Remember all that God has done for you and that you are divinely guided."*

The legal battle ensued. My attorney filed a response to the court, and a hearing date was set. Walking into the courthouse in Santa Monica two months later, I saw him in the hallway. Everything in me wanted to confront him, but I had prayed before stepping out of my car, asking for strength and guidance. In the courtroom, the judge dismissed the case, instructing us to attend mediation.

The mediation room was enormous, and we sat on opposite sides. I looked at him, not with anger but with a hope that he would understand. I spoke calmly, *"Please, I know you're young, but have some integrity. You are more than that app. You're making short-term decisions that could have long-term consequences. Love yourself more."* With that, I thanked the mediator and left, feeling a profound sense of relief. The case was dismissed, and I had said my piece. I didn't want him back; I just wanted to remind him of his worth. Integrity is all we have in this world.

The ordeal had left me drained. I reached out to my family, trying to explain what had happened, but found no solace. My boss, compassionate and understanding, allowed me to take two months off to regain my footing. I spent time in London with a dear friend, embracing the opportunity to cry, heal, and rejuvenate. We did yoga, ate nourishing food, and slowly, I began to feel like myself again.

Upon my return to California, I made a promise to explore more on my own, to find joy in the little things. I visited Ojai, a quaint and beautiful place, then traveled to Las Vegas to see Celine Dion, one of my favorite artists. From there, I drove to Palm Springs and stayed at The Parker Hotel, a place that had always felt like a haven to me. It was here that I met people who had gone through their own storms similar to mine. In those shared stories, I found a reminder: life happens to all of us. It's not about what happens but how we handle it.

I could have chosen rage, but what would that have solved? Instead, I chose to realign my soul. Travel, music, the arts—ballet, opera, theater—all of these brought me back to my center. Nature, the smell of the outdoors, being on a plane, or a boat, these moments reconnected me to myself.

At the end of 2017, I began to rebuild my life piece by piece, feeling an overwhelming sense of gratitude to return to the work I loved. My career had always been a source of joy, and I considered myself truly blessed to have a job that connected me with incredible people from all walks of life. Chloe', with its magnetic energy, seemed to attract such diversity, drawing together stories, experiences, and connections in a way that felt almost magical.

It was during one of my workdays that I met a client who would later become a very close friend. She was a powerful and well-known figure in California, someone whose presence commanded attention. During her in-store VIP experience, we found ourselves exchanging stories, diving into a genuine and heartfelt conversation that felt more like old friends catching up than a typical client interaction. By the end of our time together, we exchanged personal numbers— something I rarely did, as I typically kept a firm boundary between my personal and professional life. But there was something different about her, something in her energy and the depth of our exchange that felt profound. We clicked in a way that was both surprising and natural, and I couldn't help but feel as though the universe had brought her into my life for a reason.

Having taken two months off prior to this moment, I could almost hear the universe whispering to me: It's okay to open up again—not everyone is bad. Slowly but surely, I began to trust in that message, allowing myself to let my guard down and welcome people into my life again. That moment marked not just a return to work, but a return to connection, to vulnerability, and to believing in the good that exists in others.

The Transition Unveiled & The Blessing Embraced

This chapter was a true test of my strength and integrity. Amidst the storm of emotions, I was forced to confront the person I once loved, not with bitterness, but with a desire to seek closure and maintain my own dignity. It was through this painful episode that I learned to stand firm in my values, even when it seemed like the world was crumbling around me. The blessing came in the form of self-realization—that even in the face of betrayal and public exposure, I held the power to define my journey. In seeking solace in travel, the arts, and new friendships, I rediscovered a part of myself that had been buried beneath layers of hurt. The transition was not just about moving on; it was about embracing the strength that comes from remaining true to oneself amidst the trials of life.

Journal Entry

2018

By 2018, it had been three years since I made Los Angeles my home, and I had become adept at navigating this vast city. When I first transitioned here, I couldn't have imagined feeling this level of comfort, yet here I was. By this time, I had been promoted at Chloe', a milestone that allowed me to handle my financial responsibilities on my own with out worry of any kind, especially after the painful breakup that left me emotionally and financially strained. But now, I had found a groove, a sense of self-sufficiency.

In the world of Hollywood and luxury, I started to became a familiar face, part of the crowd that was frequently invited to exclusive events. It's not a term I enjoy using, but I had access to a level of society that most only see on social media or on television. I was ushered into private spaces, homes of celebrities and powerful people who valued their privacy as much as I did. It was a delicate dance, understanding that this access came with a major responsibility. Being invited into these circles wasn't by chance—it was a testament to the trust they placed in me, a private person who understood the value of discretion.

My promotion at Chloe' was a true blessing, opening doors for me to explore deeper complexities about myself, both professionally and personally. It gave me the chance to fine-tune my career path in ways I hadn't before, pushing me to grow and adapt in an industry that thrives on constant evolution. I was profoundly grateful for the leadership opportunities and partnerships I was now building, connections that felt meaningful and purposeful. Not for a single moment did I ever dread stepping into the workplace—it felt like an extension of who I was becoming.

This new role also brought with it a whirlwind of executive events: mingling with CEOs, executives, and celebrities, while observing the unspoken dynamics of power at play. The glittering veneer of these inner circles initially fascinated me, but over time, I began to notice an unsettling trend. Many of the individuals in positions of power were surrounded by "yes people"—those who affirmed and encouraged every decision without question. This lack of accountability often enabled behavior that was, quite frankly, far from normal. As I attended more events, it became clear that many of these "yes people" were on payroll, financially bound to validate and protect these powerful figures at all costs.

I knew deep down that I could never be one of those people. I stood firm on my morals, grounded in the belief that what's right is right and what's wrong is wrong, no matter the circumstances. While I was confident my promotion wasn't in jeopardy, I couldn't shake the lingering thought: How long will these invitations last? I knew that my refusal to compromise my integrity would set me apart in ways that might not always align with this world of unspoken rules. Still, I remained steadfast, unwilling to sacrifice my values for access, status, or approval. For me, success had to mean staying true to myself, no matter how tempting or glamorous the surroundings might be.

Truly, I wasn't judging; it was more of an observation. The more I saw, the more I realized that I didn't fit into this mold. My authenticity didn't quite match the environment where many seemed to be *"getting dressed for job interviews,"* as opposed to just enjoying the moment. It wasn't the world I had imagined when I first moved to LA. I had hoped for spaces filled with genuine connection, laughter, dancing, and music—where the weight of the day could be shed, not spaces where every interaction felt like a transaction.

Slowly, I began to distance myself from these circles. It wasn't an overnight decision but a gradual realization that I needed to find environments that resonated with my core values. I explored other ways to meet like-minded individuals, joining yoga groups and social media communities. One of these was an interior design Facebook group, where I met someone who would become a pivotal figure in my life. He was younger, and given my past experience, I was immediately hesitant. But, there was something different about him. He came from a similar background, one of humble beginnings and hard work— I admired that a lot. Over time, he became my best friend, embodying the qualities I had been seeking in people within the industry but never found.

Our friendship grew naturally, and for a brief period, we explored dating. However, I quickly realized that what I valued most was the deep, intellectual connection we had as friends. It was a conscious decision to step back from the romantic aspect and cherish the friendship we had built. In him, I found a non-industry friend who brought balance to my life—a reminder that authenticity and genuine connection could still be found in LA.

As summer approached that year, we had planned a month-long trip to celebrate my 32nd birthday. Although we decided to remain friends and not date, I still wanted to make the most of this trip. Unfortunately, because of his work—he couldn't attend. So, I invited my dear friend from Boston, who opened her home to me when I needed it most, to join me instead. Together, we embarked on a journey I had always dreamed of: exploring New Zealand, Australia, and Fiji. Those four weeks were transformative. New Zealand captivated me with its simplicity, its fresh food, and its effortless embrace of nature. We sailed to Queenstown, a private paradise, where life felt unburdened by materialistic desires.

It was a stark contrast to the world I had temporarily left behind in Los Angeles. There, we would journal, sipping the finest rosé, reflecting on how different life was outside the United States. I felt a profound connection to the simplicity and richness of life in those places. It was a reminder that life could be lived fully without the constant need for validation or climbing social ladders.

Although I didn't want this trip of a lifetime to end, I knew it was time to return to Los Angeles, where a major event at work awaited me. As I settled into the 11-hour plane ride back, carrying every emotion and memory from those four transformative weeks abroad, allowing them to linger before shifting my mindset back into work mode. Chloe' was preparing for a monumental event in partnership with the MOCA art museum, a collaboration that would merge the worlds of art and fashion in a way that promised to be unforgettable.

Before my vacation, we had sent over 2,000 invitations to an exclusive list of clients, powerful individuals, and influencers, so I already knew the preparation was going to be intense. Upon my return, I immediately dived into reviewing the invitations, responses, and the finalized attendee list. The excitement was palpable—our efforts had paid off, and we had received confirmations from some truly extraordinary people. This event was going to be significant not only for the brand but also for me in my new role. I was eager to see the vision come to life, to witness the seamless blend of art and fashion, and to feel the energy of what I knew would be a defining moment for everyone involved.

The night of the event was a whirlwind (to say the least). As we danced and celebrated the successful evening, a client whom became a dear friend, approached me on the dance floor with an opportunity. She whispered, she had been observing me during her visits to Chloe' and wanted to know if I would consider spearheading her business. It wasn't the first time someone had approached me with such an offer, but this time, it felt different. Over the years, I had been approached multiple times to assist with startups and small businesses— but, I always denied. While it was flattering, the thought of leaving the security of my established career was a bit scary.

I was proud of the stability I had built for myself—my 401(k), my insurance, my steady income. So, the idea of stepping into the unpredictable world of consulting was daunting. As we continued to speak on the dance floor, I felt a mixture of humility and fear. I told her I needed time to think it over, especially with the holidays approaching.

With that said, this particular holiday became a time of deep reflection for me—a season not just of celebration but of wrestling with a decision that felt monumental. I found myself grappling with the idea of leaving behind the career I had painstakingly built to join the startup. The thought consumed my nights, robbing me of sleep as I weighed the risks of stepping into something entirely new. Stories from friends, colleagues, and others I admired played on repeat in my mind—tales of leaps into the unknown, of joining fledgling companies with potential but no guarantees. Those stories always came with cautionary undertones, reminders of the risks involved, and the lingering question: What if it all falls apart?

Yet, amidst the doubt, another voice emerged—one far more profound. It was the voice of God reminding me of a truth that had been a constant in my life: *my journey has always been one of transition.* Change was not unfamiliar territory for me; it was woven into the fabric of my being. That voice carried an assurance, a challenge even: *If you've made it through every transition so far, why would this be any different?* You now have the tools to navigate uncertainty and bounce back, no matter the outcome.

As I leaned into that revelation, I realized that if I were to take this leap of faith, I needed to be intentional about preserving my identity. It couldn't be lost in the brands, companies, and partnerships I would inevitably collaborate with. Over the course of that holiday season, I started to dream—not just about joining the startup but about building something uniquely my own. The idea of having a personal foundation to stand on began to take root. My initials, JVB, kept coming to mind, echoing like a mantra, growing louder and more defined with each passing day.

At first, I toyed with the name "JVB Consultants," but it didn't sit right. It felt like a promise of a team I didn't yet have—a plural that wasn't true to the solitary vision I was crafting. Then came "JVB Consulting Firm," but it felt too corporate, too disconnected from my authentic self. One evening, as I was driving down the 405 in Los Angeles, the answer finally came to me. It wasn't grand or complicated; it was simple, clear, and undeniable. The universe whispered, Consult. That's what people are asking you to do. Just consult. And with that, JVB Consults became more than an idea—it became a name that carried the weight of purpose.

I didn't officially start the business right then and there, but in that moment, I knew the path was laid out before me. The clarity I had been searching for finally arrived, and the voice from the universe made everything feel... right.

The Transition Unveiled & The Blessing Embraced

In 2018, the glitz and allure of Los Angeles presented a fork in the road: to blend into the crowd or to remain true to myself. This chapter of my life unveiled a crucial transition—the realization that authenticity is often tested in environments that prioritize appearance over substance. The blessing within this journey was the clarity it brought. I learned to navigate a world filled with glamour without losing sight of my values. By stepping away from superficiality and embracing genuine connections, I found a deeper sense of purpose. This year became a testament to the power of inner resolve, setting the stage for the next steps toward embracing the risk and reward of forging my own path.

Journal Entry

2019

Well, 2019 is here and I found myself navigating a sea of life lessons through a process of trial and error. There is something about being the first in your immediate family to break certain barriers that brings a unique loneliness. When you venture into uncharted territory, seeking guidance from those who have never left their own familiar bubbles becomes almost impossible. It's not a matter of judgment, but simply the reality of our different experiences. It's like trying to discuss the complexities of marriage with someone who has never been married—they can listen, but they can't truly comprehend the nuances. That was my reality at the close of 2018, leaving me confused about whom to turn to for advice as it pertained to me departing corporate america after many years.

Yes, I was surrounded by people in the industry, Hollywood, and various circles of influence, but there was something about the confirmation of family. While I was still growing in my career, constantly searching for answers, what I began to understand in 2019 was a hard pill to swallow: no one genuinely cares about your situation unless it benefits them in some way. Reflecting on this, brought back times when I had always shown up for my friendships, family, those close to me— supporting with a giving heart. There were numerous times I quietly swiped my card to help financially, and though I'll never go into detail—because I believe in protecting others' stories—I had always been there— no matter what. Now, as things started to get confusing for me, I found myself longing for that same support to be reciprocated. Although I didn't need help financially, I was still looking for the unwavering friendship and support that I had been providing. I would drop everything I was doing to be there and to show up fully in my friendships, offering my time, my energy, and my presence without hesitation. But life has a way of teaching us that sometimes, we are meant to stand on our own.

As the new year dawned, I stood at a crossroads: should I stay in corporate america, steadily climbing the ladder, or step into the unknown and embrace the life of an entrepreneur, regardless of the outcome? It was time to make a decision. I had to provide a final answer within days.

With my mind racing and me not feeling like I had the answers, I thought of my interior design friend whom I had met in the Facebook group years back. I knew he had just experienced this very thing two years prior. He too had been working in corporate america for sometime and I thought, why not try him. So, I called him.

True to his character, he spoke with conviction, sharing that he had always seen me building something for myself—a business that would reflect my vision and purpose. He encouraged me to take the leap of faith, and because I knew his values and the strength of his relationship with God, I trusted him deeply. It wasn't just what he said but how he said it—with a confidence that felt divinely inspired.

I asked if we could meet in person, and when we did, we prayed together. It was a moment of connection and surrender, a spiritual alignment that quieted all my doubts. After that prayer, something shifted within me. My soul was at ease, and the path ahead felt clear. I told myself, *"Jordan, you've got this— take the leap of faith."* And for the first time, I truly believed it.

On June 7, 2019, I handed in my resignation letter, asking the universe to guide my steps and hold my hand through this new chapter. I was nervous and scared; my heart raced with uncertainty about what lay ahead. But I knew that staying too comfortable could cause me to lose sight of my true purpose.

When I shared my decision with my boss, she was taken aback. I explained that this was not a choice I made lightly. It wasn't that there was anything wrong with my job or the company, but the incremental raises I was receiving year after year were not going to take me where I envisioned myself in the years to come. To reach my goals, I needed to be bold, to listen to the voice of the universe urging me toward entrepreneurship. I knew it was time to step into this new journey as a small business owner.

While I could see the shock still lingering on my boss's face after I handed in my resignation letter, she responded with grace. Her words of encouragement and wisdom were unexpected yet deeply appreciated. She wished me well as I prepared to embark on this new chapter, and her support became an unexpected source of reassurance. It wasn't long after that moment that my mindset began to shift. Life, as I had known it, was changing rapidly, and I had to adapt just as quickly.

One of my first steps was reaching out to the two individuals who had been waiting for me to join their team. Conversations moved swiftly, and before I knew it, the ball was rolling. I also knew from previous experiences that I needed to approach this transition with care and diligence. This time, I hired an attorney to review and redline contracts, ensuring that everything I signed would set me up for success.

During one of my early conversations with the client, I felt it was important to be completely transparent. I told them I couldn't have anticipated the magnitude of the changes 2019 was bringing, but one thing I did know was that I had already planned a trip to Mykonos, Greece, for my birthday that August.

One client in particular insisted on me starting before my trip, as they aimed to open their business by September that year. Realizing the intensity and flexibility entrepreneurship would demand, I agreed to dive right in. Starting on July 15, 2019, meant moving swiftly. However, by July 5th, right after the Fourth of July holiday, I received a call requesting that I join them for an audition for a major television show in Beverly Hills. My start date wasn't until July 15th, but I knew that in the world of entrepreneurship, flexibility was key. So, I agreed and joined them for the audition. Afterward, we discussed the tasks ahead, and it became clear that I would be taking on a monumental role, executing everything mostly on my own.

From logo design to acquiring business licenses, overseeing construction, selecting furniture, choosing paint colors, and working with the interior designer on every detail of the store layout, my responsibilities were endless. I remember pulling all-nighters, working from 6 AM until 6 AM the next day, driven by a mixture of adrenaline and determination. The pressure to create a website, build landing pages, manage social media, and hire a full staff weighed heavily on my shoulders. Yet, despite the exhaustion, I never complained. I was grateful to be working, to be trusted with this project.

As my scheduled trip to Greece approached, I started to reconsider taking the vacation. But, I had already made financial commitments for this trip— I was confused. With everything on my plate, I wondered if I could truly afford the time away. Ultimately, I went, knowing my friends would be upset if I canceled. When I arrived in Mykonos, Greece, and saw my friends, I embraced them tightly. It wasn't just because I was thrilled to be far from the United States, but because I was truly grateful to be in their presence at such a pivotal moment in my life. It was my birthday, and this trip symbolized so much more than just a celebration—it marked the beginning of a milestone journey into entrepreneurship. The beauty of the Greek islands surrounded me, and yet, I couldn't believe how much this trip had come to embody all the transitions I was navigating.

Even in the midst of paradise, my phone didn't stay silent for long. Calls, emails, and updates about projects pulled me back into the responsibilities I had left waiting across the ocean. I found myself balancing work commitments while trying to soak in the breathtaking sights of the islands. Each moment felt like a tug-of-war between my desire to be fully present and my unwavering work ethic that refused to let go.

I tried to enjoy the moments as much as I could—the sparkling blue waters, the warmth of the sun, the laughter of my friends—but my mind never strayed too far from the responsibilities waiting for me back home. That sense of dedication, of always giving my all to everything I commit to, was both my strength and my challenge. Mykonos became a poignant reminder of the duality I was learning to navigate: the need to embrace the present while carrying the weight of what lay ahead.

Upon my return, I was immediately tasked with organizing a birthday celebration that would be filmed in mid September, on top of everything else. I embraced the challenge, diving into the whirlwind of planning and execution. We were still on track for the grand opening at the end of September. Despite my exhaustion, a sense of pride grew within me. This was entirely different from the corporate world I had known, requiring a different mindset and business acumen—one that was black and white, with no room for gray areas. There were moments of doubt when I questioned if I had made the right decision. But I was not someone who gave up easily.

I knew too well the sting of being walked out on, of feeling abandoned when the going got tough. So, I committed myself fully, even as it meant spending the holidays and ringing in the New Year with the team rather than with family or friends. This was the life of an entrepreneur, a life I had chosen. It was challenging and often lonely, but it was also a testament to my resilience and willingness to pursue the life I envisioned for myself, no matter the cost.

In stepping into the unknown, I was learning to trust the process, to embrace the risks, and to honor the voice within that told me I was capable of so much more than I had allowed myself to believe. This journey was not about the destination, but about the growth and strength I was finding along the way.

The Transition Unveiled & The Blessing Embraced

2019 was a year of stepping into the unknown, a journey that tested my resolve and commitment to pursuing a life beyond the familiar. This transition unveiled the power of taking risks and trusting the voice that urged me forward. In embracing the challenges of entrepreneurship, I discovered the blessing of resilience and the courage to redefine what success meant to me. The blessing here was not found in the achievements themselves, but in the growth, the strength, and the unwavering belief that I could carve a path uniquely my own.

Journal Entry

2020

By 2020, my name had begun to circulate throughout Los Angeles and even stretched across California. Whether it was my connection to a well-known individual or simply the strength of my work ethic, I started to see doors opening in ways I hadn't anticipated. One of my clients, in particular, was instrumental in creating opportunities that expanded my entrepreneurial journey. Calls and emails started coming in more frequently, as people began to take notice of the dedication and excellence I brought to my work.

I'd be lying if I said I wasn't tempted to take on more clients. The allure of growth and the validation that came with new opportunities were hard to resist. But deep down, I knew that the clients I already had were all I needed at that moment. It became clear to me that navigating this new world of entrepreneurship wasn't just about saying "yes" to every opportunity—it was about protecting the integrity of my work and the relationships I had already cultivated.

It was also during this time that I began to understand the importance of boundaries—both in entrepreneurship and in life. The line between personal and professional often blurs in this world, and it's rarely encouraged to prioritize anything other than the grind. Entrepreneurship, by its very nature, demands nonstop effort, and it's easy to lose yourself in the pursuit of success.

But I made the difficult decision to say "no" to new clients, even when the opportunities were enticing. It wasn't easy, but it was necessary. I needed to stay loyal and steadfast to the commitments I had already made, ensuring that the work on my plate reflected the best of who I was. This lesson in discipline and balance would become one of the most important cornerstones of my entrepreneurial journey.

Despite the constant influx of calls, texts, and emails—even after I had said no—I knew it was time to take the next step in my entrepreneurial journey. That step was rooted in an idea that had been brewing since the year prior: JVB Consults. With everything moving so quickly and my name beginning to reach new circles, I recognized that this wasn't just about growth anymore. It was about protection. It was time to safeguard my intellectual property—the essence of my creativity and vision.

I've always been a person full of ideas, but now, with the guidance of my attorneys, I was learning an essential truth: I no longer worked for a company—I was the company. Every idea, every phone call, every email was an extension of my business. It was a shift in mindset that demanded intentionality and vigilance. My attorneys emphasized this to me repeatedly: *"Your intellectual property is your greatest asset. Protect it."* Their words became my mantra.

In 2020, I started taking this to heart. While I remained committed to the work already on my plate, I also focused on ensuring that I, as an entity and a creator, was protected. JVB Consults was no longer just an idea floating in my mind—it became official. With the help of my legal team, it was solidified in documents, a tangible representation of what I had birthed within me: creativity, resilience, and vision.

And then, as if the world itself was waiting for this moment of alignment, the unthinkable happened. The COVID-19 pandemic struck, bringing with it a global shutdown that no one could have foreseen. It was a time of uncertainty and fear, but it also reinforced why this step—protecting my ideas, my business, and myself—was so necessary.

The 2020 pandemic brought the world to its knees. The air was thick with uncertainty as we collectively tried to grasp what this meant. Was it a flu? A cold? Something more insidious? Amidst the chaos, my world didn't stop. While most were confined to their homes, adjusting to the new reality, my team and I continued to work relentlessly. There was no pause button. Projects had deadlines, events were planned, and the show had to go on.

However, three months into the pandemic, the nonstop pace took a toll and my health began to slip. Fast food became a staple, the byproduct of days where hours blurred into one another, leaving me disoriented. What day was it? Was it morning or night? I truly didn't know at times. The only constant was the looming pressure to perform. I was surrounded by a team that supported me, yet I started to realize I was extending myself way beyond the original contract's limits, taking on more than I should. During this time, my perception of business began to shift. Gone were the days of the well-oiled corporate machine, where protocols and protections were the norm. In this new world, I had to forge my own armor, to stand firm and shield myself from being exploited. It was a hard lesson to learn at the time but, I realized on this journey, it was me and me alone.

November 3, 2020, was far from just another day. It was an election year in the United States, adding a layer of tension to an already precarious time marked by the global pandemic. The day is etched in my memory not just because of the election but because that morning, as part of my routine before starting work, I took a COVID-19 test—and it came back positive.

The news hit me hard, and I knew I would need time away from everything to recover. It wasn't just the physical toll of the virus, though; it was the emotional weight of isolation that began to creep in. Like the rest of the world, I was confined to my home. There were curfews, restrictions, and constant reminders to avoid meeting up with others. The vibrant world I had once known was eerily quiet, and the silence amplified my sense of loneliness.

During those moments at home, I started to feel a deep yearning for connection, something to fill the void left by the absence of my usual social and professional interactions. That's when I decided to explore the app everyone seemed to be talking about at the time: Tinder. It wasn't just curiosity—it was a response to the solitude that came with the shutdown.

I guess, like so many others during that period, I was looking for companionship, for someone to talk to in the stillness of those long, uncertain days. My work life had shifted dramatically; gone were the predictable 9-to-5 hours. Instead, my days blurred into nights, and the boundaries between work and rest vanished completely. Amidst the relentless pace of work and the quiet of my recovery, I found myself navigating the Tinder app more frequently, searching for something— or someone—to bring a sense of connection back into my life.

Well, needless-to-say, after lots of swiping, I met someone—a wonderful man from the country of Colombia. He was in California on assignment, and our connection was immediate, yet grounded. We were very careful not to rush things, aware of the complexities of our situations and the restrictions *COVID* placed on the possibility of getting to know each other deeper. His departure back to Colombia was sudden and dictated by the world's circumstances. Despite our growing bond, I didn't have the luxury of dwelling on it at all. My plate was overflowing with responsibilities.

The holidays were approaching, and he was now back in his country, painting vivid pictures of a place I had never considered visiting. Colombia had always been a distant name, never really on my radar. But through his stories and photos he'd send via WhatsApp, I began to see it through his eyes—a country of breathtaking mountains, vibrant culture, and a people who cherished family and life's simple pleasures. He often invited me to visit, yet I hesitated. Could I really take a break? Could I step away from my responsibilities, even momentarily?

I had always carried those questions in the back of my mind—the ones that lingered, whispering doubts about whether stepping away and having free time was ever truly possible. For reasons I couldn't fully articulate then, I had been conditioned to believe that a life outside of work was a luxury I couldn't afford. Certain clients, intentionally or not, would make it clear that my dedication needed to be unwavering, as if having a personal life was nonnegotiable.

Looking back, I wish I had the courage I possess now. I wish I could have confidently shared the importance of balance, of setting boundaries, and of living a life that isn't solely defined by work. But in 2020, those lessons hadn't fully taken root in me yet. All I knew was that I needed to keep working, to stay focused, because the pandemic had upended everything. The uncertainty it brought made it feel like there was no room to slow down or risk losing momentum.

That same year, he invited me to Colombia—a chance to step away, to experience something outside the confines of work and isolation. But I didn't even allow myself to entertain the idea. Fear outweighed curiosity. The thought of losing my job or falling behind in my commitments was enough to keep me grounded, tethered to the belief that I had to keep pushing forward, no matter what. It's a decision I've often revisited, not with regret, but as a reminder of the lessons I was still learning about the value of balance and the courage it takes to claim it.

In December 2020, the world started to open up ever so slightly. With projects momentarily wrapped up, I dared to dream of a holiday escape. It was a risk, venturing to a place I knew little about, to meet someone I was still getting to know. I kept it quiet, not because I was ashamed or secretive, but because it felt too fragile to expose to the world. This was my sacred space, something I needed to protect until it was strong enough to stand on its own.

So, I went. And Colombia welcomed me with open arms. It was not just the country but the way of life that captivated me. The people there, despite having far less than many, possessed an abundance of what truly mattered—peace of mind, integrity, genuine friendships, and an unwavering love for life. It was a stark contrast to the fast-paced, often superficial existence I had been living. In Colombia, life moved at a different pace. It wasn't about the next big project or the endless chase for recognition. It was about savoring moments, appreciating the natural beauty around, and embracing the richness of simplicity.

This contrast was striking compared to my life back in the States, where I had become the emergency contact for many of my celebrity and powerful friends and clients. They excelled at projecting an image of being perfectly fine to the public, but behind the scenes, it was a different story. Late at night, I would receive phone calls and texts, urging me to come over immediately. They were battling feelings of despair, contemplating suicide, or considering leaving the industry altogether. It was a heavy reality, a constant whirlwind where peace seemed elusive, and I often found myself as the lifeline in their darkest hours.

Being in Colombia allowed me to step back, to see my life from a different perspective. My friend and I spent time together, deepening our connection, yet keeping it beautifully simple. The Colombian culture was gentle, not rushed, and it was refreshing to be in a place where everything was not about more, bigger, or faster. It was a lesson I needed—a reminder that life could be lived differently.

But as the holiday drew to a close, reality called me back. I was determined to returned to my world with a new understanding, a deepened sense of self. I had learned that boundaries are essential, that I deserved time to decompress, to live beyond the confines of my work. And even though clients inundated me with calls and messages, demanding to know every detail of my absence. What they didn't realize, was that, those very actions were pushing me closer out the door.

It wasn't just about the work; it was about respect.

As I looked back on this chapter of my life, it was not just about the discovery of a new culture or the beginning of a relationship. It was about realizing that my worth was not solely defined by what I could give to others— when they wanted it. It was about learning to balance, to draw lines, and to protect the spaces in my life that needed to remain sacred.

I returned from Colombia not just with memories, but with a renewed perspective. It was a place that taught me that true wealth is not in what you have but in who you are, how you treat others, and how you live your life. And it reminded me that amidst the chaos, it is possible to find peace, to ground yourself, and to protect the parts of your life that matter most.

The Transition Unveiled & The Blessing Embraced

The year 2020 was a profound turning point, a transition that unveiled the delicate balance between professional dedication and personal well-being. In a time when the world came to a halt, I realized that I had the power to pause, to redefine what mattered, and to carve out spaces of peace amidst the storm. The blessing was in discovering that boundaries are not walls but bridges to a more grounded, authentic life. This period taught me that protecting my inner world was not just a necessity but a sacred act of self-love.

Journal Entry

2021

Starting this journal entry, I find myself recalling the peculiar nature of 2021. It was a year shadowed by the aftermath of 2020—a time when the world had come to a sudden halt. The *COVID-19* pandemic had not just swept across the United States; it had affected the entire globe. As we all did our best to moved forward into 2021, my path forward seemed a little unclear, as I truly didn't know how life would continue following the lockdown.

I vividly remember during this period, my phone rang constantly with calls from past clients, all frantic about the direction the world was taking. There was a collective scramble to adapt—to revamp, restructure, rebrand, and re-market. The world had shifted towards a new touch-less way of living. I remember how everything changed overnight: point-of-sale devices replaced with QR codes, and the once bustling public spaces now stood eerily quiet. People were taking every precaution, hesitant to enter stores or gather in crowds.

As I mentioned in the previous journal entries, I had been fully immersed in this new venture/project; even sometimes pushing aside personal goals and boundaries I had set for myself. Friends and acquaintances were navigating their own struggles as companies laid off employees and closed entire departments. Life, as we knew it, had transformed, and yet, in 2020, I kept going. I didn't pause long enough to feel the shift. I was working nonstop, unaware of how deep the changes around me ran.

As 2021 continued on, I began to feel a shift as well—the kind the world had already endured the year prior. Maybe it was because, for the first time in a long time, my own life was beginning to make sense. I was no longer constantly stressed and I could finally breathe. But with that clarity came an unexpected wave of connection—or, perhaps, reconnection. Friends, acquaintances, even family members I hadn't spoken to in years started reaching out. They asked for help, for advice, or for guidance, and I couldn't always tell if their intentions were genuine or if they assumed I had somehow "arrived." Perhaps they thought I was now connected to a world that, in their eyes, meant I had resources to spare.

Around this same time, my face started appearing on television. People noticed. My phone rang more often, text messages poured in— not from clients, but from old friends, distant relatives, and people who seemed to emerge from the shadows of my past. I wasn't sure if it was because they saw me on their screens, or because they, like the rest of the world, were grappling with isolation. After all, 2021 was a year of solitude for many. People were spending more time at home, tethered to their mobile devices, searching for answers or connection in whatever way they could. I was just another beacon on their radar, though I couldn't yet discern if it was the light of genuine care or opportunistic convenience.

Nevertheless, I kept my thoughts to myself, assuming they were just struggling to adapt to this new reality— this new way of living. Also, around this time, the digital world had taken over like never before— Instagram, Instagram Live, Facebook, Facebook Live, TikTok, SnapChat, Twitter/X, OnlyFans, YouTube—it all seemed to explode overnight. Everyone was building a social media presence while I was still a bit caught in the whirlwind of work, constantly flying from one place to another, with no time to strategize or slow down.

It was during one of my many travels that I fell seriously ill. At first, I tried to push through it, dismissing the severity of my symptoms. After all, taking time off, even for a little while, felt impossible with the weight of my responsibilities. I had tested positive for COVID-19 the year before, so I convinced myself it couldn't possibly be that again. Maybe it was the constant flying—boarding a plane nearly every week—that was wearing me down. But the pain deepened, and my body began sending signals I could no longer ignore.

I made an appointment with my primary doctor, who ran every test under the sun. When the results came back, I was floored: I had tested positive for COVID-19 again. This time, it was more severe, and my doctor insisted I take a full week off, effective immediately. I knew I needed to listen. I knew my body needed rest, and yet, it felt unnatural to let myself pause. On some level, I feared what stepping away might mean. But with the severity of the illness, I told myself, *This time, I'll stay in bed and do nothing.*

Surprisingly, even in my vulnerable state, the calls came—endless calls. A particular client rang me only two days into my recovery, asking if I had "healed yet." Two days. Not the seven my doctor had prescribed. There was no acknowledgment of the humanity behind the work I had done or the suffering I was enduring—no regard for the larger context of what the world was enduring. It wasn't about my health or my well-being; I soon realized— it was about power, control, and deadlines.

After just three days of rest, I broke my promise to myself. I put on my gloves, masked up, and went back to work. I had to keep going— there were bills to pay, student loans waiting to be chipped away at. I ignored the exhaustion in my body and spirit and forced myself forward. I didn't give myself the grace to fully heal. Survival, at the time, seemed to mean pushing through, no matter the cost.

Returning to work, I was met with whispers, gossip, and lies swirling around me— about me. I knew their origin but chose to absorb it all, needing to understand the source motive(s). In the back of my mind— I suspected what it might have been. But, I soon realized it stemmed from my decision to keep my personal life separate from my professional one, a boundary I was well within my rights to establish.

Later that year, a client requested that I travel with them for a month—a request that was unprecedented for me. Coming from a corporate background where work had defined hours and clear boundaries, this felt entirely out of the ordinary. Yet, the entrepreneurial world I had stepped into thrived on constant emergencies, so I agreed.

Little did I know, this wasn't about urgency but rather exercising power, yet again. A client's desire to exert control.

The journey began on April 1st, taking me from New York to Alabama, with a brief return home for my sister's wedding. As the best man at her wedding, it was a sacred moment I wouldn't have missed. However, while in Alabama, I experienced some of the most degrading moments of my life. Strangers and acquaintances would quietly acknowledge the mistreatment I was facing, yet none dared to confront it openly, intimidated by the *"power"* this individual wielded.

One night, after fulfilling my responsibilities for the day, I was completely drained—physically, emotionally, and mentally. I remember being asked to do something that fell well outside the scope of my contract, and for the first time, I expressed my exhaustion and declined. It wasn't easy for me to say no, but I had nothing left to give. I retreated to my accommodations, and once I was alone, I broke down. I wept—not over the client or the situation, but over the realization of how deeply I had allowed myself to be placed in such a compromising position.

That night, I couldn't sleep. I laid awake, my mind racing as I reflected on the entire project. I began writing down everything I had done, everything that had been asked of me, and weighing the pros and cons of it all. As I reviewed my notes, one truth became painfully clear: I had been doing far more than what the contract required of me. I wasn't just fulfilling expectations; I was exceeding them to the point of self-sacrifice, and I hadn't even noticed how much I had let myself slip away in the process.

In that quiet moment of reflection, I made a decision. I told myself, *"You see this trip through because you don't walk out on something you've started. But from this point forward, you will no longer compromise your personal values for anyone."* It was a promise not just to protect myself but to honor the boundaries I had ignored for far too long. That night marked a shift—a reminder that my worth was not tied to how much of myself I gave away.

As my time in Alabama progressed, tensions began to surface. I felt them, but I chose not to dwell on them. My focus was on doing my job, fulfilling my responsibilities, and keeping my head down. Still, in the back of my mind, I was counting down the days until I could return home for something far more meaningful—my sister's wedding.

When the day finally came, I boarded the flight, utterly drained from everything I had been carrying—physically, mentally, and emotionally. I remember the sheer exhaustion. I must have fallen into the deepest sleep during that flight because, by the time we landed, the flight attendant had to gently wake me, letting me know that I had arrived. Groggy but filled with a quiet excitement, I stepped off the plane, knowing I was exactly where I needed to be. Here I was, ready to stand beside my sister on one of the most important days of her life.

My sister, like me, is part of the LGBTQ+ community, and being there as her best man meant the world to me. Especially considering our childhood, I was so happy to see her getting married, and not just getting married, but getting married to a woman. I know how hard it must have been for her to stand in her truth and marry a woman, considering our upbringing. Yet, even during this sacred family event, the client's incessant calls continued. Requests that could have waited were made with the sole purpose of asserting dominance over my life. It was relentless.

This period was transformative, not just because of the difficulties but because of the guidance I received from the man I was now dating. His words and wisdom were a balm to my troubled soul, gently reminding me of my worth. He urged me to seek help, to hire an assistant. Up until then, I had believed in the adage, *"If you want it done well, do it yourself."* But the world was changing, and so was I.

So, I took the leap and hired an assistant—a significant step in relinquishing my need to control every detail, not just in my work but in my life as well. But, who knew it came with its own challenges. The criticism from those I considered friends and family was unexpected and, frankly, disheartening. They judged me for hiring help, for making what they perceived as a "luxury" choice, without any understanding of the pressure I was under. What they didn't see was that I was drowning. I needed help to stay afloat, and their judgment only deepened the weight I was already carrying.

What amazed me most was how people reacted when my assistant reached out to them. Some automatically assumed I had changed, that hiring an assistant somehow meant I thought I was above them. In their eyes, having an assistant equated to being "on top of the world," when in reality, it simply meant I needed extra hands and extra eyes to get through one of the most stressful periods of my life. I realized then that it wasn't my place—or my responsibility—to explain the nuances of my decisions to anyone. I didn't owe them justification, nor did I want to give it.

In that moment, my definition of friendship began to shift. I started to see that true friends don't question your choices out of judgment— they support you, trust your intentions, and recognize when you're doing what's best for you. This realization was both painful and liberating, marking another turning point in how I understood the relationships in my life.

By the time I returned to Los Angeles, I was utterly exhausted. I had been away for over a month, juggling multiple clients, and struggling to recalibrate my life. For the first time, I truly began to question the path I was on. The world was still in flux, and while many were still locked down, reevaluating their lives, I had been on the go—nonstop.

The man I was dating spoke to me again, with words that cut to the core: *"You need to think about what truly matters to you. The world is changing, and I want you to live your life with purpose, not just running around making everyone else's dreams come true while yours fade away."* Those words were a wake-up call. I knew I had to make a change. On June 1, 2021, I made the decision to part ways with a particular client. It was the beginning of reclaiming my life. After parting ways with the client, I wasn't overwhelmed by a sense of loneliness, but rather by a desire to disconnect temporarily from the LA scene. I wasn't wanting to connect with anyone else in LA because it was heavily industry-driven, and that's all I was around at the time. I just wanted a different scene.

I tried to reclaim my routine—yoga, therapy, and the small comforts that had once grounded me. The man I was dating became a pillar during this time. He observed my growing discontent with California, the changes in my circle, and the weariness that had taken hold. One evening, he made a suggestion that took me by surprise. *"Jordan, you've been in LA for six and a half years. You're not happy there anymore. Come to Colombia for six months. Rejuvenate. Hike, eat healthy, focus on your mental health. Just let go and move in with me. I won't charge you anything. I just want you to sit with yourself for six months."*

His words felt like a lifeline thrown to a drowning man. I was hesitant; moving out of the country again seemed daunting, especially amidst the uncertainty brought by the pandemic. I was still managing three clients, so I didn't know how that would work. Inquisitively, I approached them about the possibility of working remotely. When they agreed, I took it as a sign from the universe— it was time for a change. As crazy as it sounds, I sold my convertible

BMW, canceled the lease on my Beverly Hills apartment, and placed most of my belongings in storage. With just six months' worth of essentials packed in three suitcases, I prepared for this new chapter.

I was so excited for the next chapter of my life as everything seemed to be falling into place perfectly. The opportunity to spend six months abroad felt like a gift—a chance to step away, recharge, and focus on my mental health. I couldn't have been more grateful for the timing. Before leaving, I was approached by two individuals I had worked with in the past. During this time, everyone was seeking new ways to generate residual income, and I was in a solid financial position with no major bills weighing me down. Their pitch was simple: invest in property. It seemed like the perfect opportunity to expand my portfolio, especially since real estate was something I had never ventured into before.

The timing felt right. I trusted these individuals, having worked with them previously, and with the prospect of additional income on the horizon, I decided to proceed. I wired my portion of the investment to them and eagerly headed off to Colombia, ready to begin my mental health retreat. For two days, I immersed myself in the peace of my new surroundings, feeling lighter than I had in years. Then, everything unraveled.

On the third day, I received a call from the bank where I had wired the funds. The representative informed me that the documents submitted by the individuals I had partnered with—tax forms, bank statements, everything—contained falsified information. The bank was freezing the account, seizing the property, and dissolving the business. The property, which would have been placed under my name, was now out of reach. My world shattered.

In a single phone call, everything I had planned, trusted, and hoped for was undone. I sat there, thousands of miles from home, grappling with the gravity of what had just happened. This wasn't just a financial loss; it was a betrayal, a harsh lesson in trust, and a cruel reminder that even the best intentions can lead to devastating outcomes.

Suddenly, the six-month mental health break I had envisioned turned into a legal and financial crisis. I reported the fraud and found myself entangled in police reports and legal battles. Arriving in Colombia, I was not the person I had hoped to be. I was facing devastation, unsure how to navigate this new reality. My finances were wiped out; my savings and 401(k) cashed out. I was at rock bottom.

Desperation led me to reach out to everyone in my phone and email box. I was growing scared. I swallowed my pride, reaching out to friends, family, and acquaintances, hoping for immediate support. But, to my shock, many of those I once considered close made excuses, leaving me in disbelief. It was a painful reminder of the fragility of relationships and the isolating nature of crisis.

Here I was, in Colombia, trying to navigate the mess of it all from a distance. My Colombian, with his seemingly endless well of care and positivity, had already prearranged a routine for me to help me heal— a mix of hikes, yoga sessions, and even connecting me with a therapist I would see three times a week. I wanted to tell him immediately about the devastating news that had been weighing on my soul, but I hesitated. Our relationship was still fresh, too new for the kind of emotional load I was carrying. I didn't want his light, his positive energy, to dim under the weight of my truth. So, for two months, I went along to get along, silently carrying my burden while showing up for the activities he set forth.

One morning, during one of our many hikes, my body betrayed me. We had been climbing steadily when I started to feel strange, my limbs growing light, almost as if I no longer had control over them. I knew I had been under immense stress—burying so much deep within me that I hadn't shared—but, as with everything in my life, I convinced myself I could keep going. I could hold it all together. As we made our way back down the hill, dizziness swirled in my head, and the world went dark. I collapsed, hitting my head on the cobblestone. The last thing I remembered was falling—then waking up in a hospital bed.

The doctors told me I had suffered a nervous breakdown. *"How?"* I asked. I am only 35 years old. They warned that if I didn't begin to take care of myself, things would only get worse. Lying in that hospital bed, I realized the universe had spoken to me—this time, not in a whisper but with a roar. It wasn't just a fall. It was a reckoning, a bold and unapologetic message that something had to change. This was yet another transition, another moment of upheaval, and though I was shaken, I knew it wasn't just a collapse. It was an invitation to finally lay down the weight I'd been carrying.

I finally found the courage to confide in him, revealing the full extent of my situation. My nerves were frayed as I spoke, unsure of how he would react. Our relationship was still so fresh, and to be honest, I had grown accustomed to people walking in and out of my life. I truly believed this would be no different. But to my surprise, he didn't leave. He didn't retreat. Instead, he stood by my side, unwavering in his support. Despite his own responsibilities—his work, his commitments, his life in his own country—he made me his priority. He ensured the doctors understood exactly what I needed and when I needed it. He even bridged the gap of language, helping me navigate conversations. His presence was steady and constant, and it was unlike anything I had ever experienced before.

You have to understand—I grew up not knowing what true love looked like. I had spent most of my life afraid of trusting it, afraid of embracing it. Yet, here it was, staring back at me in ways that softened the walls I had built around my heart. This man's love wasn't fleeting, conditional, or performative. It was real, and it brought us closer than I ever could have imagined. Life has a way of revealing itself in the most unexpected ways. What began as a moment of collapse, became a moment of connection, teaching me that even in my darkest hours, I was not as alone as I thought.

Still, as I lay in that hospital bed, I wrestled with a mix of emotions. Embarrassment clung to me like a shadow. I had reached out to so many people, asking for help in ways that felt vulnerable and desperate, only to be met with silence by some. I was sure they thought I was crazy—that someone who seemingly had it all together could suddenly unravel. I had to face not only my feelings about the situation but also the rejection that came with it. I had to forgive those who didn't respond, those who ignored my calls, those who denied me when I needed them most.

But more importantly, I had to forgive myself. Life, I realized, is full of rock bottoms. It's not the fall that defines us but the way we choose to rise from it. I knew I couldn't control how others showed up for me, but I could control how I showed up for myself. And as I laid there, I began to understand that this was my opportunity—not to drown in shame or regret but to find strength in my vulnerability and take the first steps toward rising again.

By December 2021, I must say, I had finally begun to find peace with my life. I was out of the hospital, now back in his beautiful apartment that overlooked the mountains—a view so serene it felt like a balm for my soul. Life still had its uncertainties, but I was learning to breathe again. One day, out of nowhere, he told me he had taken the day off work. That alone was strange—he never took time off. He mentioned he would accompany me to my appointment with the doctor at 1 PM.

As we rode through the city on his motorcycle—one of the most common ways to get around in Colombia—I noticed we were taking a different route. It wasn't the usual path to the doctor's office, and before I could ask, we pulled up to one of our favorite restaurants. "Let's grab a bite to eat before the appointment," he said with a casualness that didn't hint at what was to come. I followed him inside, unsuspecting, only to find that he had arranged the most beautiful lunch. As the meal wound down, he pulled out a ring and proposed.

In that moment, I couldn't grasp what was happening. I couldn't breathe. I was in disbelief, overwhelmed by how someone could see a future with me—especially now, when my life felt like such a fragile, complicated mess. Sure, we had known each other for some time now, but with everything I was carrying, I couldn't fathom how he could look at me and see forever. My immediate reaction was to ask him, "Why?" It was the only thing I could think to say.

His response left me undone. *"What made me propose to you,"* he began, *"was the fact that you didn't hide from what was happening to you. You were honest and told me the truth. You allowed me to experience it with you. I witnessed your vulnerability and your willingness to include me in your life, and that showed me the true person you are. That's why I want you in mine."*

I sat there, stunned, trying to process his words. This year had brought so many twists, turns, and upheavals that it was hard to absorb what was happening. What I did know, though, was that for the first time, someone was showing up for me in a way I had never experienced before. He wasn't just speaking the words; he was living them. I've always believed that actions speak louder than words, and here he was, proving it to me over and over again. And in that moment, I began to realize what it truly meant to have someone choose you—not just in spite of your struggles, but because of the person those struggles had revealed you to be.

The Transition Unveiled & The Blessing Embraced

2021 was a year that brought a storm of changes, pushing me into the depths of my own resilience. In the face of betrayal, loneliness, and a financial blow that could have broken me, I was forced to confront not only the external forces that sought to bring me down but also the internal beliefs I held about myself, my boundaries, and my worth. This chapter saw the unraveling of what I thought was stability and the painful realization of who and what truly mattered in my life.

The transition lay in letting go—letting go of toxic relationships, societal expectations, and even the life I had built in Los Angeles. It was a journey from a place of loss to one of profound vulnerability and truth. The blessing came not from the resolutions or the outcomes but from the raw authenticity that emerged in the process. I learned to seek and accept help, to honor my need for healing, and to value my own well-being over others' perceptions. In the crucible of this turmoil, I found the unwavering support of love, not in the places I had expected, but in the quiet, steadfast presence of someone who saw me at my lowest and chose to stay.

This chapter was not just about survival; it was about embracing the gift of starting over. It was a transition into a deeper understanding of my worth, the courage to pursue peace over perfection, and the wisdom to discern the voices that truly had my best interest at heart. The chaos of 2021 stripped away illusions, leaving behind the blessing of clarity and the strength to build a life grounded in authenticity and love.

Journal Entry

2022

As I write, erase, rewrite, delete, and write again— literally in that order. My emotions are everywhere. *Where do I even begin?* You've already read about the proposal on December 21, 2021, so you can understand why I keep stumbling over the opening of this entry. Joy, happiness, excitement—those emotions were all there, mixed with the weight of everything else still looming over me. An engagement ring on my finger signified a new chapter in my life, yet I was still entangled in the legal matters surrounding the investment property that never became mine. I had to let the legal process take its course. It was hard as I wanted it to be over already— but....

In February 2022, my now fiancé received an unexpected, yet, exciting call from the company he was working with during the pandemic. They had been given clearance to resume the project that had been on hold due to the lockdown. My thoughts raced as I was only supposed to be in Colombia for six months, a time meant for healing and self-discovery. Instead, I had faced numerous challenges, which felt like I had no break at all. In my mind, I was hoping to stay longer but, now, the prospect of returning to the United States hung in the air—a place I had just left, still burdened with unresolved issues.

March 2022 marked the seventh month of my stay in Colombia, extending a journey that was only supposed to last six. He hadn't provided an answer to the company that wanted him to continue with the project. So, I was left to live in a state of limbo, but we continued to make the most of life in Colombia in the meantime. I knew, deep in my heart, that I would stand by his side no matter what decision he made. He had been my anchor during some of my darkest times, and I felt it was only right to support him in the same unwavering way he had supported me.

I didn't pressure him. I didn't try to persuade him one way or the other or make him feel guilty for whatever choice he was leaning toward. Still, in the back of my mind, I wrestled with my own emotions. If he decided to stay, I would be relieved—I truly wasn't ready to return to the States.

The biggest emotion I wrestled with during this time wasn't joy or relief—it was the weight of uncertainty. The idea of transitioning back to the States with someone else, rather than on my own, lingered heavily in my mind. When I originally set out on this retreat—this self-healing journey—I had envisioned it as a solo chapter, a time to rebuild. I had let go of my apartment and sold my car, not as acts of loss, but as steps toward renewal. That apartment had become a symbol of the pain and upheaval I'd endured years earlier. When returning to Los Angeles— I wanted a clean slate: a new home, a fresh outlook, and the freedom to start over on my terms.

Letting go of my car had been hard, but I told myself it was temporary, something easily replaceable. What I hadn't accounted for was the shift in dynamics—this time, I wouldn't be transitioning alone. The thought of returning with someone else meant reimagining how I would navigate this next chapter. I knew what starting over in Los Angeles would require: finding a new apartment, securing a car, settling into a new rhythm. But now, I'd also have to lean on support until all the pieces fell into place—applications submitted, purchases made, plans solidified.

I kept turning over questions in my mind. Who could I call for help? Where would we stay in the meantime? After all, Los Angeles had always been my home, a place where I had defined and redefined myself over the years. Returning as part of a *"we"* rather than an *"I"* felt unfamiliar— but, I was't afraid of either outcome.

Within two weeks, he had made the decision, and it was— yes—he took the job. I began reaching out to contacts in my phone, cautious of who I could trust. My mind, catching up with reality— I guess I'm moving back. What scared me the most was, I was entering back into the States with major legal issues hanging over my head. An 85 page NDA I had signed limited what I could share/say and to whom I could say it. I had contacted a newer acquaintance, someone I knew through another friend. This person had their own ties to the industry, but despite my reservations, I opened up anyway; sharing documents, screenshots, and the full scope of what was happening. Ultimately, he helped me financially secure a way back to the U.S., as I had truly hit rock bottom.

Through conversations, it didn't take long to realize he was in a similar place to where I had once been—still entangled in the industry's allure, unable to speak his truth to his friends. He needed the *"powerful"* people more than he needed his own authenticity. I truly felt for him, recognizing a reflection of my own past struggles in this area. But, as I stated, he extended a helping hand when I needed it most— and I was truly grateful. To be honest, I hadn't expected it— not from him.

During one of our calls, one thing caught me off guard— his request for secrecy. He wanted this to stay between us, away from the eyes and ears of the very people who connected us, the inner circle that had shaped so much of our friendship. It made me pause. *Was this about discretion, or was there something deeper?* We agreed on the terms and they were simple: once these legal matters were behind me, everything would be repaid. He was fine with that, unbothered by the timeline or the weight of it. But as I walked away from that conversation, I couldn't shake the lingering question: If someone is willing to help you, yet unwilling to be seen doing so, what does that say about the nature of your bond? I didn't question in the moment, I was just grateful for the help, as I transitioned back to California.

In the desperation of finding a temporary place to stay, with time slipping through my fingers, I reached out to a friend I thought I could trust—someone who had been an integral part of my journey in Los Angeles. She was someone I felt I could open up to, despite the immense pressures I was facing. But from the moment we reconnected, something felt off. Our conversations lacked the warmth and familiarity they once held. It struck me as strange; I'd only been away for seven months, but it was as though something had shifted between us, though I couldn't quite put my finger on what it was.

Still, I needed help during this transition, so I pressed on, candidly sharing my situation. As we spoke, it became clear that her pursuit of the *American Dream*—complete with the husband, the baby, and the white picket fence—had reshaped her identity. The person I once knew had been overshadowed by this new version of herself, a version I struggled to connect with. Yet, despite this transformation, she agreed to let us use her home as a transitional space.

Her three-bedroom home in Los Angeles was beautiful, a place I had visited countless times before her shift in priorities. For years, it had been a refuge for me, especially during some of my darkest moments in LA. I had memories of late-night talks, laughter, and the kind of support that made me feel grounded in an otherwise turbulent city.

When my fiancé and I arrived, her demeanor was so off-putting. The friend I once knew was gone, replaced by someone guarded and distant. It was a sobering moment. Her definition of friendship and mine were worlds apart. I found myself questioning everything while standing in her space with our four suitcases. The joy I felt about sharing this new journey with my fiancé was overshadowed by the uncomfortable reality of our situation. She exuded a closed-mindedness toward our cultural differences, a stark contrast to the open acceptance I had come to embrace.

My fiancé sensed it too. The atmosphere in the house was tense, making it difficult for him to sleep or feel settled. He was trying to find his footing for his new work project while we were simultaneously searching for an apartment and looking to buy a car. Los Angeles demanded mobility, and our transition from one country to another was proving to be more challenging than I had anticipated. My once dear friend seemed to be making it harder than necessary, despite the fact that her beautiful home could easily accommodate us.

I couldn't understand why. When she had been going through her own turmoil, I had shown up without question, because that's what friends do. You show up, no questions asked. But here we were, and her support was not what I had expected.

During this time, my fiancé's discomfort grew, and the strain began to affect our relationship. The tension in the house was palpable. We tried to make the best of it, cooking dinners for our host—my supposed friend. Yet, she would often show up late without so much as an apology, acting as if our efforts and presence were an inconvenience. I barely recognized her anymore. It was as though the person I had once called a friend had transformed into someone else entirely.

This transition back to a place I had called home for six years quickly revealed a harsh reality: *I had nowhere to go and no one to truly count on.* The people I had known were mostly industry friends— acquaintances who drove the latest cars but lived with multiple roommates, unable or unwilling to offer a helping hand when I needed it most. I was learning some bitter truths about my past connections.

In an effect to change atmosphere, I reached out to more people, even those I had hoped to avoid. My fiancé had already fronted numerous expenses due to my poor investment decisions and mounting legal fees. The more he saw my so-called friends' reluctance to help, the more he felt incapable, not just as my partner but as a man. It was taking a toll on him, and I could feel the weight of his frustration and disappointment.

However, things were taking longer than expected. Applications we'd submitted yielded no responses, and our next steps felt uncertain. So, I kindly asked for a one-week extension. Her response, however, left me completely stunned. Instead of understanding, she demanded a fee for our continued stay. I couldn't believe it. We had already given her money when we first arrived—something that had seemed a little odd at the time but manageable given our circumstances. Now, this new demand felt not only shocking but completely out of character for her. It was as if I didn't recognize the person standing in front of me.

As I sat with this moment, I realized something deeper was at play. She seemed changed—someone I once knew as strong and independent now appeared distant and controlled, as though someone else's influence had shifted her priorities. I wanted to ask her more, to understand what was really going on, but my own exhaustion and hurt were overwhelming. The weight of her actions, and the implications of what they meant for our relationship, was a pill I couldn't yet swallow.

Out of options, and unable to stay in her home a moment longer, I made the difficult decision to leave. For four nights, we moved into a hotel. The stay was temporary but disorienting, like free-falling without a parachute. From that room, I called everyone I knew in the city—anyone who might offer a lifeline. Yet the silence on the other end of those calls was deafening. There was no one. Absolutely no one.

I had once thrived in this city. Now, I felt unmoored, as if the universe was testing my endurance and spirit, yet again. Each unanswered call was a reminder of the isolation I felt and the unpredictable nature of depending on others. But deep down, I knew one thing: I couldn't stay in a place where trust and admiration had been replaced with demands and disillusionment.

The strain began to unravel the love and solace my fiancé and I had found in each other. His productivity suffered, as did his focus on his work project. We had come to California with hope, but now it seemed like the place was stripping us of everything, including our relationship. In a heartbreaking decision, we parted ways in the very city where everything had started. I was devastated. Once again, something precious had been destroyed by the circumstances and the people who had let us down.

Now, I truly found myself beyond rock bottom. I was newly engaged, and that too had failed. I had reached out to people I once would have never confided in, exposing my vulnerabilities, only to be met with judgment and indifference. Sitting alone in that hotel room, I reflected on how far I had fallen. Just a short time ago, I had lived in a beautiful apartment in Beverly Hills; now, I was reduced to seeking shelter wherever I could find it.

Sitting in that hotel room, I couldn't stop reflecting on the realization that came from my friend—the one who had initially offered her home. I knew I shouldn't be spending my energy on these thoughts. I was no longer staying under her roof, and my focus should have been on the next step forward. But I couldn't shake the disbelief. At my very lowest, she had asked for compensation to extend our stay. And when I refused, she retaliated in ways that shocked me to my core.

It wasn't just the demand for money that stung—it was what came after. She took to spreading awful rumors about me, sending direct messages to people on Instagram and emailing my business partners with fabricated stories that were outright lies. What surprised me most wasn't just her actions but how easily others accepted her words without questioning me, first. Without seeking clarity, they believed her version of events as if it were gospel.

I guess that's the world we live in—a world where a so-called *"celebrity"* deliberate words can shape perceptions without the need for truth. Her behavior revealed so much about her character, who she truly was at her core. She thought she could isolate me, convince others to unfollow me, unfriend me, and abandon me. She tried to knock me down, but she underestimated the strength I carry within.

She must not have known my true story—what I've endured, what I've overcome—because if she had, she'd have known this wouldn't break me. If anything, it only made me stronger. Her actions confirmed what I needed to see: *she was never a real friend.* A real friend would know my resilience. A real friend would have stood by me, not tried to tear me down, when I'm already at my lowest.

I realized then that her issues were not my demons to confront. She had allowed me to experience one of the lowest points of my life with callousness that was hard to comprehend. It was a bitter pill to swallow, but it marked yet another turning point in my journey—a lesson in discerning true friendship from superficial alliances.

Although my fiancé and I had agreed not to call off the engagement, we decided to separate for a while. He remained in LA, and I was left to navigate this storm on my own. What had begun as a mental break, filled with the joy of our engagement and the excitement of his new job, had spiraled into something far more isolating and painful. This memoir is about: *Transition: The Blessing of Change,* and *Finding Strength* within that change. Yet, during this period, I was struggling to find my own strength amidst the relentless waves of upheaval.

I continued to reach out, calling and texting anyone who might help. But there came a point when I had to check out of the hotel, left with no option but to seek refuge in a shelter for three days. Here I was, in the very city I had called home for six years, a place where I had built a life that, I once thought, would never require me to rely on others. But one bad investment decision had stripped away that illusion, exposing all the cracks and faults in the life I had constructed. I don't blame anyone else for this. I have always believed in taking full responsibility for my actions and learning from the universe's lessons.

As I sat in the shelter, the universe's teachings became clearer. It was over. Everything I had once believed about friendship, success, and security was shattered. I had been in rooms most people only dream of, had conversations with individuals whose names carried weight, but none of that mattered here. Here, *it was just me,* stripped of all the trappings of my past life. In those three days, I began to see things for what they truly were. The universe had put me in this space to confront myself, to face the raw truth of my reality without any distractions.

It was during this time that I started receiving calls from my mom. Our relationship had always been rocky, but she began relaying the rumors circulating about me—how I was supposedly on drugs, losing my mind. I was, and still am, shocked by how quickly people latched onto the gossip. The reality was that no one called me to ask what was happening. Not one person sought the truth directly from me. Instead, they fed on the sensationalized stories, the headlines that they found more palatable than the truth.

This memoir is about how my life can serve as a lesson to others. I'm not sharing these experiences to play the victim but to show that even in the darkest of times, you must keep going. You may be in the midst of a tunnel that seems endless and suffocating, but there is always a light, even if it's just a glimmer. Sitting in that shelter for those three days, this was the thought that kept me moving forward.

I will never forget the moment one of my clients, whom I was still working with remotely, noticed that something had changed in me. Out of the three clients, she was the one who sensed that things had shifted. Though she was careful not to intrude on my personal life, she asked if everything was alright. Her transparency caught me off guard. In that moment, I felt like I needed to be honest.

I disclosed everything to her, laying bare the turmoil I had been navigating. I had reached a point where I knew holding back could mean missing out on a blessing. Sharing the truth with her turned out to be a pivotal moment in my life.

During our conversation, she told me she could hear it in my voice—
the exhaustion, the weight I was carrying from life's endless
demands. She saw right through the façade I'd been trying to
maintain. Her words hit me hard: *"Now is not the time to be in Los
Angeles, chasing industry help from industry people."*

At the end of our meeting, she looked at me with a clarity I didn't yet
have for myself and told me to call my fiancé. She urged me to tell
him that it was time for us to leave Los Angeles, that this city wasn't
the right place for us at this moment in our journey. Her words were
the confirmation of a truth I had been carrying silently but hadn't
been ready to face.

As soon as she said it, I broke down and cried—tears I had been
holding in for far too long. I felt the truth of her words deep within
me. I had known it all along. Los Angeles had become a space of
struggle, not opportunity, for me this time around. Yet, I had stayed,
in part, because I knew how much it mattered to him. He wanted to
show up for his work, his dreams, in the best way possible, and I
didn't want to stand in the way of that.

But in that moment, I realized something important: *sometimes the
most courageous decision isn't staying where you are but, recognizing
when it's time to leave.* And as painful as it was, I knew she was right.

She took us to Van Nuys private airport in Los Angeles, California. I
remember her telling me never to speak about the favor she was
about to do for us. She was heading to visit her daughter in college in
Virginia, and offered to drop us off in Baltimore. Her words were
direct: *"You need to be with your mom. She's the only one who will open
her arms during this time."* It was an unexpected kindness, and though
we had only a professional relationship, she seemed to understand
my situation on a deeper level.

My fiancé was by my side, although visibly unsettled. I knew he was
only there because of the love he still held for me, and I wasn't sure
how long he would stay, given his own commitments. However,
seeing him again brought a sense of relief I hadn't felt in a long time.

During the flight, my client shared her wisdom about the industry and about living one's purpose in life. She was a woman who had achieved a certain level of success, and she spoke candidly about her journey. She revealed that, in her climb, she often tried to help everyone, believing they had her best interests at heart. Without delving into specifics, she hinted at the countless challenges she had faced. Her words stayed with me: *"Keep your head down, stay true to your purpose. Sit with yourself. Figure out what brings you happiness. If it makes you smile or gives you chills, that's your purpose."*

We landed in Maryland, and as we stepped off the plane, my fiancé and I embraced, tears mingling with relief. Despite the rocky terrain our relationship had traveled, he was still my fiancé. We found refuge with my aunt for a short time before moving to my maternal grandmother's house. There, we finally began to find some semblance of peace. We made a vow to each other: *to avoid talking about our troubles for a while, to just hold each other, be intimate, and focus on the present.*

This decision brought us closer. It was one of the best choices we could have made. When we eventually felt ready to discuss the reasons for our separation, he opened up. He said he wanted to reconnect with the unwavering, bold, hardworking, and authentic person he had met years ago. Hearing those words, I knew they rang true. But they also stung, because they highlighted how far I had strayed from myself amidst everything that had happened.

This chapter of my life had stripped me down to the core, but it also set the stage for a rebuilding—one that would require confronting the truths about who I was and who I wanted to become.

During this time, while staying with my grandmother (whom I was beginning to know more about), felt surreal. In the back of my mind, I began to hear the universe whisper: *"Connect with the source of the trauma."* My grandmother was the matriarch, the origin of the family dynamic that shaped my mother, my aunts, and uncles. It was here that I started to learn more about my family's history, the parts no one had ever spoken of openly.

As I listened to her stories, the idea of generational curses began to make sense. Many shy away from the concept, but for the first time, I truly understood why, at this stage in my life, I was facing these challenges. Staying at my grandmother's house—someone I had never had a close relationship with—offered an unexpected window into my family's past. She had never been a present grandmother, always occupied with her own life. Whether that was right or wrong, I don't know. But I was grateful to finally hear her side of things, to understand where I came from.

Hearing her talk about the past and how she did her best to raise my mother gave me a new perspective. It wasn't about justifying the past, but, understanding it. It made me realize that people are often doing the best they can with the tools they've been given. Somehow, with this realization, pieces of my life began to fall into place. It felt like I had traveled around the world only to end up back at the source, to finally see the full picture.

Just as I was starting to connect these dots, my fiancé told me he needed to leave. He had sacrificed so much already, and though I desperately wanted to go with him, I knew it wasn't possible. I was tied down by ongoing legal matters, court dates, and the aftermath of my poor investment decision. So, I chose to stay in Baltimore and work through these challenges, providing the courts with documents, transcripts, additional bank statements and evidence they requested.

In preparation for recovering, I was advised to obtain fresh copies of my key documents—my social security card, birth certificate, and driver's license. It was suggested that starting fresh with updated records would help streamline the process as I moved forward. However, one day, in the midst of this effort, I received a call from The Department of Health. They informed me that while attempting to process my new birth certificate, they noticed there was no father listed on my original one. It felt like yet another blow, another burden added to the pile. How could I possibly deal with another issue. Another problem.

I immediately called my mother, seeking answers. She disclosed that she had allowed my uncle to name me because of their close relationship, and that fact that my *'father'* was unavailable on the day of my birth. Her words left me reeling— I could hardy breath. I didn't know what to believe. My so-called father was no longer around to ask, and my mother's version of events clashed with the narrative I had held onto my entire life.

My mind was spinning. I wanted to talk to my fiancé about it, but I knew he was already overwhelmed with everything we had been through. Not-to-mention, he was already back in his country navigating life again. Thankfully, my best friend Sam was in Baltimore at the time, and I rushed to her home, desperate for support. She helped guide me through the next steps, offering the stability I desperately needed. It truly was too much at this point. It was becoming increasingly clear that I couldn't trust the story my immediate family had told me. I had always believed my father had given me my name, but learning that this wasn't the case, shattered yet another illusion.

In that moment, I won't lie—I started to question God. I questioned if he was even real, because there was no way a loving God would allow me to carry this level of weight in a single year. For three days, I cried nonstop. Each tear seemed to bring a small measure of clarity, but it also confirmed what I already knew deep down: it was time for a change. It was time to take control of my life and shape it into the one I truly wanted.

So, I made a decision. I no longer wanted to hold on to a name given by an uncle who, if I'm being honest, had always brought a sense of confusion into my life—and perhaps even jealousy toward me. It was time to let go of a past dictated by others and reclaim my identity. I chose to change my middle name. I chose to change the phone number I'd held onto for years. It was time for a full cleanse—a complete transformation—and I was ready to embrace it.

I knew this was the universe way of prompting me to break free. What were the odds that I would be staying at my grandmother's home, the very root of my family's history, when all of this came to light? With my fiancé by my side— virtually, I began to see the beauty in this painful journey. Through it all, I became *Jordan Victor Brown*. And in taking that name, I made a vow: this new identity would not carry the same story as the one I had left behind.

The Transition Unveiled & The Blessing Embraced

Chapter 2022 was a profound journey of unraveling and rebuilding. It was a year that stripped away the remaining layers of illusion and forced me to confront the deepest truths about myself, my relationships, and my origins. From the pain of separation with my fiancé and the betrayal of friends, to the reconnection with my family's complex history, every experience became a thread in the tapestry of my transformation.

The transition lay in the shedding of the old narratives that no longer served me. It involved standing at the precipice of my identity and deciding to step into the unknown. As I learned more about the generational wounds that had shaped me, I began to understand that my journey was not just about personal struggles but about breaking free from cycles that had bound my family for generations. This realization was both painful and liberating. It brought to light the strength required to forge a new path, to define who I am on my own terms.

The blessing came in the form of clarity and purpose. In the midst of losing what I thought were vital parts of my life—be it friendships, my engagement, or my old identity—I discovered the resilience within me. The turmoil pushed me to embrace the unknown and to redefine my sense of self. I found the courage to change my name, to let go of attachments that no longer aligned with who I was becoming. I learned that my worth was not tied to the people who failed to support me or the name given to me without my consent.

Through this tumultuous year, I realized that my story was not bound by the past. I had the power to rewrite it. The transition was not about the losses but about what those losses made room for: a new beginning, a reclaimed identity, and a profound understanding that every moment of pain and confusion was guiding me toward my true purpose. In embracing this change, I found a strength I never knew I had—a strength that would carry me forward into the next chapter of my life with unwavering resolve.

Journal Entry

2023

I was so thankful for another year as I truly didn't think I would make it to see it. Many take this for granted, but they shouldn't. Each year on this beautiful planet is a gift, a chance to reflect, learn, and grow. As 2023 began, I found myself grappling with an array of emotions—anger, disappointment, betrayal—stemming from everything I had endured. I was approaching the final court appearance regarding the bad investment that had upended my life.

In January 2023, I prepared for this pivotal moment, dressing sharply for what would be a Zoom court appearance, a remnant of the *COVID* era. Although it wasn't a traditional courtroom setting, I wanted to present myself at my best. As the judge spoke, he expressed sympathy for what I had been through and acknowledged the long journey it had taken to reach a resolution. In that moment, I felt an urge to tell him, *"You have no idea what I've endured—the losses, the betrayals, the depths I've fallen to."* Yet, I also wanted to share the wisdom I had gained as well, the newfound strength that had emerged from the fires of change.

The judgment ruled in my favor, just as I had anticipated— however, I just didn't know when I'd see the victory. But, as the weight of that victory settled in, I couldn't help but think about the friends who weren't there to witness it. If only they had stuck around, if only they had stayed through the storm, would this moment feel different? Would life be different? The thought lingered, bittersweet, but the answer came quietly, as it always does. This wasn't about their absence—it was about my growth.

Looking back, I understand now that the universe was refining me, taking me through the fire to shed everything that no longer served me: friendships, family, situations, even the outdated versions of myself. It wasn't about loss; it was about alignment. The fire, though *very* painful, was necessary. It cleared the way for clarity and transformation, forcing me to release what held me back. And while I am certain this was the path I needed to take, I'd be lying if I said I never think about it. The ghosts of what was—and what could have been—still cross my mind.

Even so, I've learned to embrace what remains: a deep, unshakable strength and the understanding that I am exactly where I am meant to be. This victory, like so many others in my life, isn't just a testament to what I've achieved but also to what I've survived. It is proof that the journey, though painful at times, is always worth it.

It was during the final court appearance that I made a vow to myself: to go silent for awhile, to focus solely on what lay ahead, not on the past that had nearly broken me. The universe had guided me through the fire, brought me face-to-face with the source of my trauma, and delivered a resolution to what had driven me to rock bottom. Now, it was my turn to carry forward with unwavering tunnel vision, free from the distractions of others' perceptions or judgments—especially from those who never took the time to seek the truth directly from me.

I emerged from this chapter as a better man, shaped by the hard-earned lessons and the resilience I had cultivated. To truly embrace this transformation, I decided to go to therapy twice a week for a full year. I needed to dig deep and understand what the universe was trying to teach me through all this turmoil. What is my purpose? What truly makes me happy? What legacy do I want to leave behind? I realized that whenever I strayed from my true path, the universe would make things uncomfortable for me, pushing me back toward my authentic purpose.

Through therapy and engaging with like-minded individuals, I began to uncover that purpose. I realized I wanted to continue offering my business consulting services through *JVB Consults,* drawing on my experiences to guide others. Life's challenges are not meant to be kept private, but shared so that others can learn and grow through them.

I also started to reflect on how different my life could have been if I had received the proper guidance from birth. That realization led me to establish *JVB Cares Foundation,* a space dedicated to supporting mental health and ensuring that no child feels like an afterthought. Every child deserves a clear and nurturing path, shaped by parents who understand the importance of mental well-being.

I also envisioned gathering friends in a beautiful setting to discuss past traumas and current struggles over delicious food and wine. This vision gave birth to *JVB Wines.* My new initials became the foundation of my life's purpose—each endeavor a reflection of the lessons and passions that emerged from my journey.

As I sit here now, reflecting on this year, I want you to know that you can find your purpose too. If you're reading this memoir, understand that it is possible to transform your pain into purpose. You may be a private person, as I once was, but stepping into your truth can open doors you never imagined. Don't give up on yourself. You may hear voices of doubt, but push through them and pursue what sets your soul on fire.

For the entirety of 2023, I kept my head down and focused on my purpose. I listened to the voices of the universe and, for the first time in my life, consulted no one else. I turned within, finding the power that had been within me all along.

The Transition Unveiled & The Blessing Embraced

Chapter 2023 was a year of quiet resolve and deep introspection. It marked the closing of a tumultuous chapter in my life and the beginning of a new one grounded in purpose and clarity. This year was about reclaiming my power, not through external validation or achievements, but through an internal journey of healing and understanding. The transition lay in the act of turning inward—choosing silence over chaos, introspection over reaction.

The universe had guided me through the fire, showing me that the path to peace was not about seeking answers from the world around me but finding them within myself. The blessing came in the form of a renewed sense of self, a clarity about my purpose, and a resolve to live authentically. Therapy became a vital tool in this process, helping me untangle the complex web of emotions, expectations, and past traumas that had clouded my vision.

In embracing my purpose, I found the strength to transform my initials—JVB—into symbols of my mission in life. *JVB Consults, JVB Cares Foundation,* and *JVB Wines* each became extensions of my journey, embodying the lessons learned and the passion I discovered along the way. The greatest blessing was the realization that my life's experiences, both the pain and the triumphs, were not meant to be hidden but shared to inspire and guide others.

This chapter taught me the power of focus and the importance of living in alignment with one's true purpose. It reaffirmed that life's most challenging moments often carry the seeds of our greatest growth. The universe had stripped away all distractions, leaving me with a singular truth: that my purpose was not just to survive the storms, but to thrive and help others find their way through theirs.

In the silence of 2023, I found my voice, and with it, the courage to live a life that honors the lessons of the past while embracing the possibilities of the future.

Journal Entry

2024

Reflecting on 2024, I find myself filled with a profound sense of pride. As I look back over the year, I realize that doing the work—truly committing to my growth—made all the difference. As I mentioned in a previous entry, I made a vow to stick to this new path, a path that feels like a blessing, a gift of alignment and purpose. And I kept that promise to myself. But, as with any significant transformation, it didn't come without its share of challenges.

Of course, the whispers came, as they always do—rumors, speculation, chatter. *"Where's Jordan? I haven't heard from him. I haven't seen him."* It reached me, but this time, I did something I had never done before: I chose not to acknowledge it. That decision changed everything. Here's the truth I've come to understand— whatever you feed, grows. If you water a plant you don't want, it will thrive, even if it doesn't serve you. I refused to give energy to anything that didn't align with my peace or my purpose. And in doing so, I discovered something extraordinary: *the power of silence, the joy of focus, and the freedom that comes with letting go of the unnecessary.*

The past two years have brought me an unmatched sense of peace and joy, and 2024 became the year I truly began to live in it.

Mid-year, I received an unexpected email from an individual whom I had met during my hectic work life in 2019. At the time, I was engrossed in the busyness of life, and our connection didn't go beyond that initial meeting. His message came out of the blue, and he shared that he had been quietly observing my new journey. He had visited each of my business websites, done his research, and asked a simple but poignant question: *"Has something shifted in your life?"* He noted how I was now pouring energy and focus into myself— unlike the past. I acknowledged that this shift was indeed taking place. In our email exchanges, I opened up to him about how life's most challenging times often teach us the most, even when we can't see it while we're in the midst of the struggle.

Hesitant, he revealed that we shared similar stories, particularly in redefining ourselves. He spoke about how standing firm in one's beliefs can come at a cost, but the rewards on the other side are immeasurable. His words struck a chord within me. There were so many moments when I felt like giving up, moments when I was tempted to lash out, to tell my side of the story on social media, to let the world know what was really happening. But his encouragement reminded me that holding on to integrity and resilience often leads to unexpected opportunities.

Through consistent dialogue with this genius businessman, I discovered not only an ally but a new mentor. It's remarkable how you never truly know who's watching—not in a critical way, but in a way that reminds you why staying focused and continuing forward is so important. You never know who's taking note, who's being inspired, or who sees something in you that you haven't yet realized in yourself.

Our conversations deepened over time, and I began to pick his brain (always with his permission.) To my surprise, he willingly shared wisdom and insights, dropping gems I didn't even know I needed.

Then, during one of those mentorship moments, he revealed something that left me speechless. He explained that, after many successful business ventures and the heartbreaking loss of his wife, his sole purpose now was to uplift others and invest in those whose potential he believed in. With sincerity and conviction, he told me he wanted to invest in every single business venture I was building.

In that moment, I broke down in tears. The truth is, in life, all anyone really wants is to be seen, to be heard, and to know that their voice, their work, and their presence have meaning. His words (in that moment) affirmed all of that for me. Of course, he was wise enough to suggest we formalize everything, and we both signed a contract after my attorney reviewed every detail. It was a reminder of the balance between trust and accountability, emotion and professionalism.

His wisdom and generosity, coupled with our shared experiences, created a bond of trust and understanding I never imagined finding in another person. In him, I gained not only a mentor but someone who genuinely believed in my vision and my purpose. It was a gift far greater than the investment itself—it was the reassurance that I was seen, heard, and valued. And that is priceless.

He would continuously apologize for everything I had gone through but assured me that it was time for me to relax, to have creative fun, and to pursue what I should have been doing all along. His words, combined with the unwavering support of my dear cousin Sierra Watties, gave me the strength to begin writing this memoir. It was time to stop hiding behind the shadows of my private world and to share my story with the world.

With his support, I assembled an incredible creative team—a business manager, a certified personal accountant, a manager, an agent, and a brilliant social media team. Through this journey, I've learned that you can't do it all on your own. Life's challenges and traumas don't mean you should give up on yourself. I am living proof of that truth. Just as I was embracing this new chapter of joy and opportunity, life took another turn.

My beloved cousin Sierra took her final breath, leaving me devastated. Yet, amidst the grief, I felt grateful for the time we had to privately grow our relationship. I am thankful that our last conversation ended with a promise to her: that I would write this memoir as she wanted me to.

The Transition Unveiled & The Blessing Embraced

2024 was a year that tested my resolve and challenged my very core, yet it also became the foundation of my rebirth. This chapter of my life unveiled the transition from a place of turmoil and uncertainty to one of clarity, purpose, and support. The blessing behind this transition was the realization that struggles can become the very catalyst for growth. The year taught me that resilience, integrity, and the courage to share one's story can open doors I never knew existed. In embracing the power of community and the value of investing in others, I found the strength to continue the race, carrying forward the legacy of my cousin Sierra and the wisdom of those who believed in me.

Journal Entry

2025

2025, marks my last year in my 30s, amazed at how life unfolds when you remain open and refuse to let bitterness take root. This entry might be brief, as this memoir is set to release in 2025, and my journey, as far as this book is concerned, is still unfolding. Yet, it's my hope that by walking you through my life journey, I've shown that you can go through anything and still emerge on the other side stronger and wiser.

Facing life head-on, without succumbing to the noise and opinions of others, has been a pivotal lesson. Staying focused, rooted in my values, and grounded in my morals, goals, and integrity has guided me through every challenge. It's crucial never to let anyone take you out of character. I never imagined I'd be here, writing my memoir, fully embracing what brings me joy. I've learned to live not for others but for myself, pursuing what aligns with my authentic purpose.

Being unapologetically in your purpose is a gift we all have the right to experience, but it's not one that comes easily. It requires dedication, resilience, an unshakable commitment to oneself, and the courage to tell the truth about who you are—no matter how messy, raw, or vulnerable that truth might be. The journey isn't free of challenges; in fact, I know more will come my way. But this time, I'm ready. The toolbox I now possess is equipped with everything I need to face them head-on.

As I look toward 2025, I'm stepping into a year of being unapologetically me—a version of myself that has emerged through every trial, every moment of self-reflection, and every ounce of work I've poured into this path. Writing this memoir allowed me to lay my soul bare, to unearth the truths I'd buried, and to find freedom in the process. My hope is that this memoir becomes a beacon for anyone who feels stuck, lost, or unable to move forward. If it can show even one person that change is possible, that resilience can be built, and that joy can be found on the other side of pain, then every word was worth writing.

My milestone 40's await in 2026, I feel ready to start this next chapter of life equipped with a new set of tools that only my past experiences could have provided. I want to encourage you not to lose sight of your purpose. It's not about what has happened to you, but how you choose to move forward.

Through all of this, I've learned the importance of self-love and self-care. As you navigate your own *change and transitions*, take care of your heart and your spirit. Be kind to yourself in moments of struggle, and seek help when the weight becomes too heavy to bear alone. There is no weakness in reaching out; in fact, it is a profound act of courage. You deserve the space to heal, to grow, and to thrive.

This is not an end, but a continuation. As I move forward, I carry with me the lessons learned, the love shared, and the promise that every new beginning is a chance to find a deeper sense of self. May we all continue to embrace the *transitions and change* that shape us, nurturing ourselves with love, care, and the strength to seek support when needed. In every step, may we find: *The Blessing of Transition and Strength In Change.*

The Transition Unveiled & The Blessing Embraced

My Daily Mantra:

Be Kind To Yourself. Be Patient With Yourself.
You Only Get One Temple.

The Blessing Of Transition:

FINDING STRENGTH IN CHANGE

For Permission Requests, Write To The
Publisher At The Address Below:

JVB Consults LLC

458 North Doheny Drive. #69189

West Hollywood, CA 90048

(E) info@jvbconsults.com

International Standard Book Number (ISBN)

979-8-218-52374-9

Library of Congress Control Number (LCCN)

2024920263

The Blessing Of Transition:
FINDING STRENGTH IN CHANGE

 @JordanVictorBrown

 Jordan Victor Brown

 @JordanVictorBrown

 www.JordanVictorBrown.com